CO-ACTORSHIP IN THE DEVELOPMENT OF EUROPEAN LAW-MAKING

CO-ACTORSHIP IN THE DEVELOPMENT OF EUROPEAN LAW-MAKING

The Quality of European Legislation and Its Implementation
and Application in the National Legal Order

Ernst M.H. Hirsch Ballin
and
Linda A.J. Senden

T·M·C·ASSER PRESS

Published by T.M.C. ASSER PRESS
P.O.Box 16163, 2500 BD The Hague, The Netherlands
<www.asserpress.nl>

T.M.C. ASSER PRESS English language books are distributed exclusively by
Cambridge University Press, The Edinburgh Building, Shaftesbury Road,
Cambridge CB2 2RU, UK,
or,
for customers in the USA, Canada and Mexico:
Cambridge University Press, 100 Brook Hill Drive, West Nyack, NY 10994-2133, USA
<www.cambridge.org>

ISBN 90-6704-184-X / 9789067041843

PREFACE

Unity in diversity is a feature of the European Union in which 25 countries, each with its own national legal order, come together in a single European legal order.

The European Union is not an arbitrary forum for cooperation but a legal order that applies to all its actors – EU institutions, Member States and citizens. The European legal order serves the EU's diversity and plurality, and the EU legislature must take this into account.

European legislation is not intended to detract from the diversity of legal traditions, methods and systems in the Member States, but rather to shape their compatibility. European legislation therefore never stands alone but must always be considered and applied in balanced cohesion with the applicable national legislation.

Just as the EU's legislature must serve diversity and plurality, so must national legislatures increasingly be mindful of their roles as part of a single European legislative process. With time, achieving and maintaining the delicate balance between unity and diversity increasingly becomes a shared responsibility of the EU and national legislatures, just as the subsequent uniform application of European law is a shared responsibility of the EU and national courts.

National legislatures and courts are not only *consumers* of European law, and as such subject to its binding force, but are also *co-actors* in the development of the manifold interlaced legal systems of the Member States and the European Union.

It is in this context that the 19th colloquium of the Association of the Councils of State and the Supreme Administrative Jurisdictions of the European Union – whose General Report you have in front of you – should be understood.

The colloquium produced several interesting conclusions which are set out in the report. It also played a role in a process in which the bodies responsible for advising governments on legislation and the Union's administrative courts are developing a greater awareness of their position as co-actors in the formation of European law. In this process, it is important to continue striving to achieve and preserve a balance between unity and diversity. The balance is embodied in the connecting links between Community law and national law. In these connecting links, the co-actors must always play their own roles and counter the many forces that may disturb this delicate balance.

The colloquium and this report represent only one moment in the process which I very much hope can and will be pursued in the framework of the Association, on the basis of 'the spirit of The Hague'.

I should like to address a word of thanks to the general rapporteur of the colloquium, Professor Ernst Hirsch Ballin of the Dutch Council of State, who presided over the substantive preparations for the colloquium, and to Professor Linda Senden, who wrote the report. I should also like to thank those who assisted them and the staff of the Dutch Council of State.

Finally, thanks are due to the national rapporteurs, since it is their reports that provided the foundations for this colloquium and General Report.

December 2004   Herman Tjeenk Willink
Vice-President of the Dutch Council of State

TABLE OF CONTENTS

Part I

Reflections on Co-Actorship in the Development of European Law-Making

ERNST M.H. HIRSCH BALLIN

Part II

General Report. The Quality of European Legislation and Its Implementation and Application in the National Legal Order

LINDA A.J. SENDEN

Chapter 1
INTRODUCTION

Chapter 2
INTERPRETATION OF EUROPEAN LEGISLATION IN THE MEMBER STATES

Chapter 3
CONCLUSIONS AND SOLUTIONS

Annexes

LIST OF ABBREVIATIONS

BOE	Boletín Oficial del Estado
BverwG	Bundesverwaltungsgericht
C.E.	Conseil d'Etat
CFI	Court of First Instance
CMLR	Common Market Law Reports
CMLRev.	Common Market Law Review
ConstEur	Treaty Establishing a Constitution for Europe
ECHR	European Convention on Human Rights
ECJ	European Court of Justice
ECR	European Court Reports
ELRev.	European Law Review
EP	European Parliament
ESF	European Social Fund
EU	European Union
EuLR	European Law Reports
EWHC	England and Wales High Court (Administrative Court)
IGC	Intergovernmental Conference
JRP	Journal für Rechtspolitik
MP	Member of Parliament
MEP	Member of the European Parliament
NGO	Non-governmental Organisation
NVwZ	Neue Zeitschrift für Verwaltungsrecht
OJ	Official Journal
OMC	Open method of coordination
STC	Simon's Tax Cases
TEC	Treaty establishing the European Community
TEU	Treaty on European Union
UKHL	United Kingdom House of Lords
VAT	Value Added Tax

PART I

Reflections on Co-Actorship in the Development of European Law-making

ERNST M.H. HIRSCH BALLIN[*]

* President of the Administrative Jurisdiction Division of the Dutch Council of State and Professor of International Law, Tilburg University, The Netherlands. The author thanks Johan van Haersolte, staff member specialised in EU law, for many valuable remarks and suggestions. He is grateful to Herman Tjeenk Willink, Linda Senden and Molle Eisma for stimulating discussions about the subject of the colloquium and their comments on the manuscript.

1. INTRODUCTION

The topic of the 2004 Colloquium of the Association of the Councils of State and Supreme Administrative Jurisdictions of the European Union ('the European Association') was not, on the face of it, very original. It was hardly the first meeting devoted to the quality of European legislation.[1] However, the focus of the colloquium – including the questionnaire, the workshops, the national reports, the reports by judges at the Court of Justice of the European Communities ('ECJ') and the Court of First Instance ('CFI') and the General Report written by Linda Senden – was a new one, namely, the work of the supreme national administrative courts and advisory bodies on legislative matters that belong to the European Association. This work is shaped ever more strongly by the requirements of national constitutions and the constantly developing legal order of the European Union ('EU').

Along with the General Report included in this publication,[2] a CD-ROM edition of the reports from the national institutions, ECJ and CFI is being released. Those reports form the background and basis for the reflections below. Unsurprisingly, the preliminary rulings procedure features prominently in them, because it is the primary connection between the work of supreme national courts and that of the supreme EU court. Even so, as I explain below, it is not the only interconnection of this kind and can by no means be seen in isolation from the others.

It has often been noted that interconnections are a characteristic political mechanism in the European constitutional order – which consists of the written and unwritten rules and principles not only of the European Union/European Community but also of the Member States and their autonomous components, such as *Länder* and *regioni*.[3] In this article, however, I focus on the relevance of interconnections to deconcentrated responsibility for the identification of relevant sources of law and for the development of the law. As the analysis below demonstrates, an array of interactions integrates the European and national le-

---

[1] Cf., e.g., *Simple is Better – Effective Regulation for a Competitive Europe*, conference of 7-8 October 2004, Amsterdam; the European Commission's Action Plan, *Simplifying and improving the regulatory environment*, COM(2002) 278 final; 'Kwaliteit van de Europese regels' (Symposium of 5 April 2001), Dutch Council of State 2001; *Improving the Quality of Legislation in Europe* (Conference of 23-25 April 1997), Alfred E. Kellermann et al. (eds.), Kluwer Law International 1998.

[2] The version of the General Report that appears here was revised by Linda Senden after the Colloquium.

[3] Neill Nugent, *The Government and Politics of the European Union*, 5th edn., Durham: Duke University Press 2003, p. 474.

E.M.H. Hirsch Ballin and L.A.J. Senden, Co-Actorship in the Development of European Law-Making
© 2005, T.M.C.ASSER PRESS, The Hague, The Netherlands and the Authors

gal orders into a generally well-functioning network, or in fact a network of networks.[4] Interconnections play a vital role.

The core of the analysis is that organs of the national legal order, such as the member institutions of the European Association, should not regard themselves as mere 'consumers' of EU law, but rather as co-actors in the development of the interlaced legal systems of the Member States and the EU. This insight bears on the approach these national bodies take to their judicial and (with regard to implementing legislation) advisory tasks. It also sheds light on the subtle manner in which the ECJ corrects and adjusts the application of national law. In particular, I would note the recent case law acknowledging and clarifying the role of national courts.[5] If national courts clearly understand their role, they will not request more preliminary rulings than necessary and, just as importantly, they will bear the consequences of their own errors.

2.   THE CONSTITUTIONAL FRAMEWORK

In 1983, when the Dutch constitution was rewritten, it was regarded as superfluous to make a distinction between international and European Community law with regard to enactment or application. As a result, however, of the widely discussed constitutional character of the Communities[6] – which was visible long before we started talking about a Constitution for Europe – the relationship between the legal order of the European Communities, or the European Union, and national law is fundamentally different from the relationship between international law in the traditional sense and national law.

The ECJ has played a decisive role in bringing this about. From the outset, the preliminary rulings procedure set out in the present Article 234 of the Treaty Establishing the European Community ('TEC') and Article III-369 of the Treaty Establishing a Constitution for Europe ('ConstEur'),[7] allowed the Court to *intervene systematically in the internal operations* of the Member States' legal systems. Never before had a body established by treaty been in a position to intervene to such an extent. The Court did not hesitate to invoke this author-

---

[4] E.M.H. Hirsch Ballin, *Netwerken van rechtsontwikkeling,* The Hague: Lemma 1999.

[5] ECJ case C-224/01, judgment of 30 September 2003, *Köbler*; cf., ECJ case C-453/00, judgment of 13 January 2004, *Kühne & Heitz* and ECJ case C-129/00, judgment of 9 December 2003, *Commission/Italy.*

[6] Cf., J.J.H. Weiler, *The Constitution of Europe: 'Do the new clothes have an emperor?' and other essays on European integration*, Cambridge: Cambridge University Press 1995, p. 295.

[7] This contribution follows the numbering and the text of the articles in the Treaty Establishing a Constitution for Europe (CIG 87/2/04) as signed on 29 October 2004 in Rome.

ity; at the earliest opportunity, it held that the status of Community law is itself a matter of Community law and that Community law takes precedence – 'primacy', in the terms of the ConstEur[8] – over domestic law.[9] Therefore, it is now fair to say that the ECJ has 'more powers than any other international court'.[10]

Such considerations, however, can lead to an oversimplified view of the relationship between EC/EU law and national law, and specifically to the notion that the first is hierarchically superior to the second. This view is flawed in at least three respects:

- The lawmaking institutions of the EU are not straightforwardly superior to national institutions but are in several respects dependent on them. Firstly, the EU's law-making institutions are dependent on the Council, the EU's central legislative body, which is composed of representatives from Member State governments. Secondly, in the future, the EU's legislative bodies will be dependent on the national parliaments, whose role will be strengthened by the procedure for monitoring the subsidiarity principle introduced by the ConstEur.[11]

- The principle of conferral, which was already part of Europe's constitutional framework but is now included in Article I-11 ConstEur, blocks any attempt to establish the general superiority of EU law; instead, it creates a situation in which EU law and national legal systems constantly interact with each other.

- Finally, a no less important factor is the European institutions' legitimacy gap. According to Joseph Weiler '[t]he Community has adopted constitutional practices without any underlying legitimizing constitutionalism'.[12] This legitimacy gap, along with practical constraints, will continue to play a role for the foreseeable future. The impracticability of far-reaching pan-European codes, as well as the EU's shortage of legitimacy, will subdue any temptation to impose rigorously unified European legislation. The Constitution for Europe rightly does not ignore this diversity, but seeks to make it a hallmark of unity.[13]

---

[8] Art. I-6 ConstEur.

[9] Koen Lenaerts and Piet van Nuffel, *Constitutional Law of the European Union*, London: Sweet & Maxwell 1999, pp. 505-506; ECJ case 26/62, *Van Gend & Loos*, ECR 1963, p. 3; ECJ case 6/64, *Costa/ENEL*, ECR 1964, p. 1203.

[10] Henry G. Schermers and Niels M. Blokker, *International Institutional Law: Unity within diversity*, The Hague/London/Boston: Martinus Nijhoff 1995, p. 420.

[11] Art. I-11(3) ConstEur and Protocol on the role of national parliaments in the European Union.

[12] Weiler, op. cit., n. 6, p. 298.

[13] See Art. I-8 ConstEur.

These are all indications that the relationship between EU law and national law should no longer be described in hierarchical terms, i.e., in terms of superiority and inferiority, but in terms of interaction. This interaction is what makes it possible for EU law to play its distinctive role within the Union. The defining feature of that concept is and has always been that nation-states are integrated into a European whole. But the European Communities differ from earlier projects of integration, which had relied on armed force to control nation-states; instead, the Communities involve nation-states in a growing number of common policies. It is to this end that EU law has the 'primacy' established by more than forty years of ECJ case law and now explicitly conferred by Article I-6 ConstEur. As I argue below, this primacy can be regarded as a rule of interpretation for national law, which has been 'Europeanised' in all sorts of ways. This is not equivalent to the claim that the legal order created by the founding treaties and the future ConstEur has superseded national law. The rule of primacy is not addressed to the European institutions – since from their perspective, it is superfluous – but to the Member States.

There is a hierarchy, however, within the EU's legislative system and that of the Member States, and after years of discussion, it will be codified in the ConstEur. Article I-33 ConstEur identifies three categories of European legislation: *European laws* (previously regulations), *European framework laws* (previously directives and framework decisions) and implementing legislation, known as *European regulations* (see Annex 2).

This provision finally gives form to the hierarchy of norms that has been debated ever since the preparatory work for the Treaty on European Union (TEU).[14] If, in the work of the courts, there is little need to distinguish between secondary Community legislation and delegated secondary Community legislation[15] – given that both have primacy over national legislation – this does not change the fact that the relationship between acts of parliament and delegated legislation is of great relevance to the relationship between the constitutionally mandated institutions in any legal order, including the EU's.

3.   The *Sui Generis* Nature of the EU's Legislative Procedures

On the basis of the information and conclusions in the national reports, it is possible to sketch a cyclical model of the development of EU law. This model highlights the fact that European institutions are not solely responsible for this

---

[14] See General Report, Chapter 2, section 1.2.
[15] Cf., General Report, Chapter 1, sections 1 and 2.

development, but operate in a larger network, interconnected with national legislative and judicial bodies.

European legislation is not intended to do away with the diversity of legal traditions, methods and systems in the Member States, but rather to ensure their compatibility. The values enshrined in the Treaties and the ConstEur do not require legal harmonisation as an end in itself; on the contrary, they require respect for the variety of institutional arrangements and legal cultures in the Member States, in part because this variety reflects the diversity of social structures. This respect for diversity finds expression in the principle of subsidiarity (Art. I-11 ConstEur)[16] and the various ways in which the Treaties and the ConstEur seek to strike a balance between EU powers and national powers.

That balance is at times jeopardised by conflicts between the interests of different parties (often different Member States) and by mutual distrust. The significance of central rules (in this case legislation from 'Brussels') is generally overestimated. Centralised rule-making that does not take account of genuine differences is precisely what leads to arbitrariness in the day-to-day application and enforcement of the rules. That applies nationally and *a fortiori* in the EU, because societies and legal cultures differ from country to country and the operation of EU rules must respect these differences in order to achieve results. The question is, who is to ensure that a fair balance is struck in policy on legislation, beforehand and in retrospect, and who should be involved at national and EU level?

In the context of an EU legislative policy, the question is not how many rules we need, but how much uniformity is required in order to make the EU's legal system function properly. That question repeatedly crops up when the criteria of proportionality and subsidiarity must be applied and when European legislation is drafted. The same question can be asked about the methods for national implementation of EU law and the ways national courts deal with the CILFIT doctrine.[17] The problem is that stricter standards for uniformity lead to greater strain on legislative and judicial mechanisms (including the preliminary rulings procedure), both in the Member States and the EU.

The fact that the EU's legal system is inextricably intertwined with the legal systems of the Member States is the greatest challenge facing that system. Ever

---

[16] In European political discourse, the subsidiarity principle has often been misrepresented as merely a barrier to exercising legal powers at EU level. The historical and constitutional meaning of subsidiarity is that authority should be exercised in such a way that other qualified actors remain able to contribute to the normative structure in their own manner. It follows that the subsidiarity principle is relevant not only to the question of *whether* European legislation should be enacted, but also to the questions of *who* should enact it – possibly more than one entity – and *how*.

[17] ECJ case 283/81, *CILFIT*, ECR 1982, p. 3415.

more often, the development of the law takes the form of a unified process, involving many players at both European and national level: legislative, executive and judicial authorities. For instance, European policy on legislation is made not only by the Commission but also by the Member States (both directly and through the Council), the European Parliament and the national parliaments. The administration of justice is performed jointly by the ECJ and the national courts. In this respect, they are highly interdependent.

The motto of the European Union, 'United in diversity' (Art. I-8 ConstEur), thus neatly captures the main aspiration and quality standard for European legislation. The European Union has created a highly diverse area of freedom, security and justice, with free movement of persons, goods, services and capital. As a result of the subsidiarity principle[18] and the various ways in which the founding treaties and the ConstEur seek to balance EU powers and national powers, EU legislative procedures have acquired not only their own *sui generis* character, but also an object and purpose that differ from those of national legislation.[19] One main characteristic is that it is not an independent system, but fundamentally intertwined with the legal systems of the Member States.

The other side of the coin is that the national actors in the law-making process – the legislative authorities in a broad sense, including interest groups and advisory bodies, and the judiciary – are not merely subordinate *consumers and appliers* of EU law, but contribute in their own right to the fabric of national and supranational European law. That is why I refer to EU institutions and national authorities as co-actors in European law-making, all interconnected. The EU legal system and the Member States' legal systems are interconnected through the following activities:

- preparation and drafting of European legislation (through the participation of officials and experts from the Member States);

- the EU's official legislative process (through the Council in the co-decision procedure and, in the future, through Article I-11(3) ConstEur and the Protocol on the role of national parliaments in the European Union);[20]

- implementation (national legislatures have to meet the EU's legal requirements and, if they transpose legislation incorrectly, may be subject to infringement proceedings);

---

[18] Art. I-11 ConstEur.
[19] See General Report, Chapter 1, section 2.
[20] Protocol No. 1 annexed to the Treaty Establishing a Constitution for Europe.

- the work of the national courts, who in most cases will apply EU law within the context of national law and may be under an obligation to request a preliminary ruling from the ECJ;

- the feedback from the experiences in court and legal practices to the European legislative process.

These five activities form a complete cycle of interconnected EU and national law-making. This European legislative cycle can be visualised in the following way:

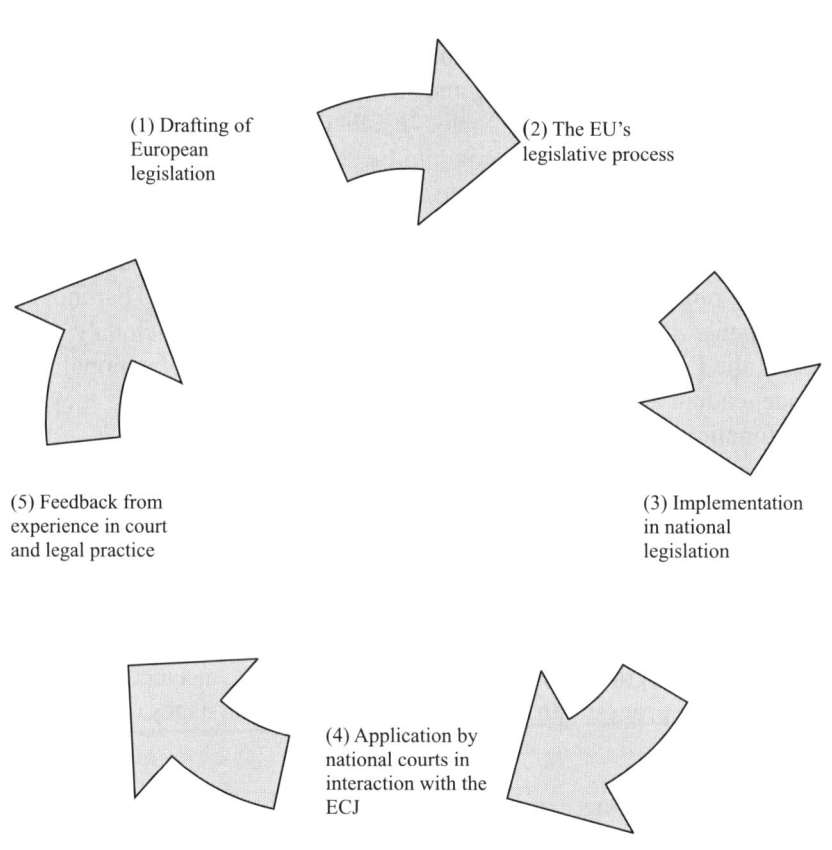

(1) Drafting of European legislation

(2) The EU's legislative process

(5) Feedback from experience in court and legal practice

(3) Implementation in national legislation

(4) Application by national courts in interaction with the ECJ

4.   CO-ACTORSHIP

There can be no doubt that EU law and the national legislation of the 25 Member States have not merged into a single legal system. On the contrary, there is a complex – but all the more valuable – network of interaction between European and national actors in the legislative and judicial branches. Within this network, law-making takes place through juridical acts some of which belong to the EU's legal order and others to the legal orders of the Member States. These interconnected acts produce a – in many respects fascinating – legislative cycle. Their interconnectedness does not detract from the distinct character of EU law-making, as compared to national procedures, but rather builds on this distinction.

This co-actorship is a feature not only of relationships between courts and relationships between legislators but also of a court system's relationship with a legislator (in the feedback stage) and the legislator's advisers on legislative matters, including a Council of State. In other traditions, an active role for judges is taboo, because the judge would be seen as misappropriating the role of legislator or politician. But the role of the national courts in the context of EU law is a special one. The national courts have acquired certain tasks directly pursuant to Community law. Those tasks, moreover, are sizeable and sweeping. In addition, Community law too is very much judge-made law. That inevitably has consequences for the mindset of judges and the way in which they operate. Because of the Europeanisation of decision-making, the role of national institutions, independent advisory bodies included, will have to change if they are to continue functioning adequately.

In so far as an interconnection is functioning well, it will support the interplay between the EU and Member State legal systems in general and thus reduce the burden on each of the other interconnections; e.g., the better the implementation of European legislation in national law, the less the risk of overstretching the preliminary rulings procedure. Although the interconnected activities depicted above represent a full cycle of the law-making process, there are other interconnections cutting across the circle. For instance, feedback to the EU legislative process can stem from any of the other stages of the cycle.

5.   WHAT DETERMINES THE QUALITY OF EUROPEAN LEGISLATION?

As noted, the quality of European legislation cannot be measured in quite the same way as that of national or sub-national legislation. Linda Senden discusses several reasons for this in the General Report. The quality of European legislation is often considered from the perspective of the national legislature whose responsibility it is to implement it in national legislation. The main question he has to tackle is how to reconcile, e.g., the directive in question with the national regime for the subject area concerned. But besides the national legislator, the national judiciary will also have to apply the European legislation, often in combination with national law. In both cases, one should realise that European legislation and national legislation may have different aims in regulating the same subject area. National legislation often predates the adoption of EU norms and therefore shapes the frame of reference of those who are confronted with EU law at the national level.[21]

The quality of legislation has traditionally been assessed 'from above', i.e., from the perspective of an authority that wishes to regulate a particular subject area. But it is also important to view it from the perspective of those who have to work with the legislation, including the courts. The effectiveness of the legislature depends on interpretation, application and enforcement. This is not a new insight. In 1313, it became clear that the continent of Europe was divided into many different states, each with its own legal order, when Holy Roman Emperor Henry VII tried – unsuccessfully – to claim general legislative powers as 'ruler of the world'. It was universally acknowledged that without effective application and enforceability, such powers were meaningless. Pope Clement V wrote in a decretal of 1314 that the jurisdiction of a prince extended no further than his power to enforce it, and Philip of Leyden (d. 1382), legal adviser to the Count of Holland, came to the same conclusion in his treatise *De cura rei publicae et sorte principantis*: 'Every duke, count or baron may be called a prince within his own jurisdiction and on his own territory'.[22] As a result of this doctrine, the political and legal unity of Europe was a lost cause for many centuries to follow.

As Europe moves towards further integration, the opposite process is now under way: when courts in the EU Member States apply European legislation, the European Union is a genuine source of public authority. That is why it is now important to view the quality of legislation from the perspective of implementation and application, particularly in the courts.

The quality of *national* legislation, from the perspective of practical implementation, relates to the legitimacy, consistency, clarity and completeness of laws. These criteria do not automatically apply when assessing the quality of *European legislation*, however. That is because of the nature of European legislation, as opposed to national public law. The national legislature's natural ambition is to provide norms governing legal relationships, but this is not the central focus of European legislation. European legislation does nevertheless have force of law within national legal systems and takes precedence over na-

---

[21] See General Report, Chapter 1, section 2.
[22] Armin Wolf, *Gesetzgebung in Europa 1100-1500, Zur Entstehung der Territorialstaaten*, Munich: Beck 1996, p. 23.

tional law. However, even when European legislation – particularly regulations – has direct effect in the sense that individuals may derive rights directly from it, the effect is complementary to that of compatible provisions of national law. In general, therefore, European legislation does not aim fully to regulate a particular subject area but to interact with national and sub-national rules.

For this reason, one should recognise that, in fact, the quality of European legislation is not manifest until it is implemented in national law, and partly depends on the national implementing legislation. In that process of implementation, national legislatures take various approaches to the architecture and terminology of European legislation.[23] But finding terminology consistent with the need to implement European legislation is a two-pronged task. In the Netherlands, for instance, some have questioned whether phrases such as *verbod van het maken van onderscheid* [prohibition on making a distinction], used in connection with the Equal Treatment Act [*Algemene wet gelijke behandeling*; AWGB], can remain in use now that more and more EU anti-discrimination legislation has to be implemented within the framework of that act. The use of this neutral term makes it necessary to make every permissible distinction explicit in the law. The method of combining a blanket prohibition on making distinctions with provisions on specific exceptions is structurally unsuitable for the EU legislature, for which it would be an impossible task to describe all the exceptions. The Dutch Council of State has therefore recommended basing implementing legislation on the term *discriminatie* [discrimination] from this point onwards.[24]

This example shows that, alongside the explicit flexibility of framework laws and the structural flexibility of soft law (legally not directly binding instruments), certain legislative techniques can be found to avoid rigidity – in particular the use of terms that are *konkretisierungsbedürftig*, though these terms must of course be sufficiently expressive. The question is whether the Bird and Habitat Directives were up to this standard, and if not, whether that might explain the uncertainties of many national legislatures. The national reports present many cases relevant to this issue.

That brings us to the question of how much uniformity is needed, a relevant question for both the EU legislature and the EU court providing preliminary rulings. This is an important point in assessing the quality of European legislation. In the field of European integration, much depends upon the effect of legal instruments, particularly legislation, judicial activity and decisions of the ex-

---

[23] See General Report Chapter 2, section 1.3.1.
[24] See the advisory reports of the Dutch Council of State on this matter, *Parliamentary Papers*, *Tweede Kamer (House of Representatives)*, 2001/2002, 28 187 A and 2002/2003, 28 770 A.

ecutive. Gráinne de Burca has pointed out that EU law cannot build on the 'underlying social solidarity' which in Emile Durkheim's view is the normal state of affairs. 'The process in the Community sometimes appears as the reverse, in which an attempt is being made to *create* solidarity through law, by declaring common principles and rights in the hope that these will influence the legal systems of the Member States as an integrating force'.[25] This view assumes even greater importance in the light of the expansion of the EU's sphere of operation and of enlargement to include a considerable number of new Member States.

The most important quality requirement for European legislation is therefore not that it be complete, but that it be capable – where necessary – of coordinating a multiplicity of national systems that will continue to exist in all their diversity.

6.   EU LAW-MAKING IS NOT JUST A MATTER FOR EUROPEAN INSTITUTIONS

The previous section refers to differences in attitude towards European legislation between national or sub-national legislators and the EU legislator. The Constitution for Europe introduces new terminology and a more uniform procedure for enacting European legislation. The relationship between European legislation and national legislation leads to an extremely specific quality requirement for European legislation, namely that it has to have sufficient 'normative flexibility'. To refer back to the motto of the European Union,[26] European legislation has no other aim than to ensure that the powers of national legislators are 'united in diversity'. This applies of course to *framework laws* as well. Article I-33, paragraph 1(3) ConstEur describes them thus: 'A European framework law shall be a legislative act binding, as to the result to be achieved, on the Member States to which it is addressed, but shall leave the national authorities the choice of form and methods'. At first sight, the situation is different when it comes to *European laws*. Article I-33, paragraph 1(2) ConstEur provides 'A European law shall be a legislative act of general application. It shall be binding in its entirety and directly applicable in all Member States'. But even European laws will hardly ever operate completely separately from a variety of national legislation. They must therefore be both clear and accessible. While the Constitution itself gives the European Parliament a role in lawmaking, the Protocol on the application of the principles of subsidiarity and

---

[25] Jo Shaw and Gillian More (eds.), *The New Legal Dynamics of European Union*, Oxford: Clarendon Press 1995.

[26] Art. I-8 ConstEur.

proportionality will allow national parliaments to demand a review of a proposal that in their opinion constitutes a breach of the principle of subsidiarity, provided the dissenting opinions represent one-third of all the votes allocated to national parliaments.[27]

Furthermore, there is a much-appreciated trend towards soft law. Instruments such as the open method of coordination, self-regulation and co-regulation have been viewed in a positive way by some national rapporteurs because they consider them as having more direct influence, being closer to some national legal systems and expressing more consensus and legitimacy.[28]

Both courts and makers of implementing legislation interpret European legislation. This is a creative process which involves a variety of participants and tools. The national legislature may be informed in advance of European legislation in the making. Sometimes advisory bodies such as the Council of State are consulted. When confronted with European legislation, both the courts and the legislature will make use of all the information at their disposal: *travaux préparatoires*, the preamble, Commission documents, different language versions, etc.[29]

But the creativity of different courts throughout the Member States must display coherence. The General Report, of course, carefully considers the question of whether more transparency in the EU's legislative procedures could promote coherence. Accessible *travaux préparatoires* are the main instrument for achieving transparency, but statements in the minutes of the Council can also be helpful. Obviously, the preliminary rulings procedure is of the utmost importance for ensuring coherent creativity on the part of national courts.

European decision-making procedures with regard to legislation are still not uniform. In particular, the role played by the participating Member States can differ; although a qualified majority in the Council of Ministers is usually sufficient, in some cases the right of veto still exists. Despite having become part of an independent, supranational legal order, Member States still see European legislation largely from the perspective of their own national legal systems. This is why the emphasis continues to be on limiting the EU's say in various subject areas, rather than establishing a common legal order based on the interplay between the EU and the Member States in a single legislative process. Many Member State representatives participating in the decision-making are driven by the desire to derive the greatest possible benefit and the least possible inconvenience from European legislation. Their frame of reference is their own national legislation, and the concepts and systems with which they are used to

---

[27] Protocol No. 2 annexed to the Treaty Establishing a Constitution for Europe.
[28] See General Report, Chapter 2, section 1.2.3.
[29] See General Report, Chapter 2, section 2.

working. On the basis of their own assessments of the forces at play and their own need for harmonisation, they strive to make the policy effects and normative content of European legislation reflect as far as possible their own national legislation, or to restrict that content as much as possible.

But European legislation needs its *own* frame of reference. A better approach might be to determine the degree to which the European common good requires statutory regulation in the policy areas at issue. The key question in European law-making should be how to make it possible for a multiplicity of national legislators to coexist in a single market and a single area of freedom, security and justice. This is no small task. It requires efforts to ensure convergence between the normative activities of at least 25 legislative authorities and governmental bodies – often even more than 25, since in federal and decentralised states EU law will largely have to be implemented at sub-national level.

This particular criterion of quality is highly relevant to both the creation and interpretation of European legislation. While national legislation often aims to cover all aspects of a subject area, that is not usually the objective of European legislation. However, the normative flexibility required by the European common good necessitates clarity as to objectives and methods, as well as the ability to adapt to a variety of national systems where possible. The best approach, in view of the aforementioned issues, may be preliminary examination of proposed European legislation at the national level.[30]

7.   THE ROLE OF THE COUNCILS OF STATE

It is clear what quality standards European legislation must meet, from the perspective of the national legislature and national courts that have to interpret it. It is through their legislation and judicial activity that European legislation is given effect. Those quality standards affect the independent state organs that make up the European Association of Councils of State and Supreme Administrative Jurisdictions both in their judicial work and – to the extent that this is part of their tradition as Councils of State – in their role as advisers on legislation and governance. Where the enactment of legislation is concerned, it is true that the Councils of State – in the Member States that have such a body – only become involved in EU law-making as advisers at the implementation stage. There are exceptions: in a small number of Member States advice may also be requested on proposed European legislation. However, only occasional use of

---

[30] See General Report, Chapter 2, section 2.1.

this option has so far been made. At the implementation stage, it is too late to have any influence on the wording of a European law or framework law. At that point, what is at stake is the way in which such a law or framework law is interpreted and put into effect. So once again the question arises: from what perspective is European legislation to be viewed? This is also relevant for the Councils of State in their advisory function. The normative flexibility which in many areas is required from European legislation strengthens the need for clear objectives and methods. One step on the way to such clarity is transparency in the legislative process. The General Report shows how useful access to the *travaux préparatoires* is considered to be.

The Constitution for Europe supports efforts to achieve greater transparency. Article I-38, paragraph 2 ConstEur and Article 5 of the Protocol on the application of the principles of subsidiarity and proportionality, respectively, require proposals for European legal acts to state the reasons on which they are based and how they comply with those principles. The clearer the objectives of an instrument are, the easier it is to deal with differences in terminology. Equivalence is not always necessary, although some national rapporteurs indicate that that would be preferable. Would it be helpful if Councils of State deliver advisory opinions on draft European legislation, or is the process in greater need of advice from specialists with different national backgrounds sharing a non-national view on European legislation, e.g., a European Council on Legislation as suggested in an article written by Sandström?[31] Will relying more heavily on soft law lessen the burden of implementation?

The implementation of European legislation seems to differ greatly among the Member States. Here again questions arise concerning best practices, not only from the point of view of speedy implementation, but also from that of reliable application. Judicial experience sheds light on the question of whether implementing national legislation has resolved tensions between, for instance, the terminology of European legislation and that of national legislation, or rather passed these on to the bodies in charge of application and adjudication; the national reports reveal different experiences in this respect. At the implementation stage, there are very different approaches in different Member States – and sometimes within a single state. Member States might benefit from willingness to learn from each other.

The General Report concludes that the problems that arise in the national context originate both in the European and national legal systems and in the fact that these systems still are not very well geared to one another. In this context, a distinction has to be made between the process that leads to the en-

---

[31] Cf., G. Sandström in *CMLRev.* 40: 1307-1313, 2003.

actment of European legislation and its implementation. As to the former, a relevant question – also for the new Member States – is whether it will be possible to outline best practices regarding participation in the drafting of European legislation. This concerns not only the number of participants in the drafting and decision-making procedures and their qualifications, but their attitude and their understanding of the significance and distinctive character of European legislation. European legislation is not necessarily better if it resembles national legislation.

The other side of the coin is that questions now regularly arise as to whether national legislation operates within the boundaries drawn by European legislation. The procedure created to make sure that it does – preliminary rulings by the ECJ – is one of the interconnections in the network of co-actorship.

8.   THE CONTRIBUTION OF THE NATIONAL COURTS TO THE QUALITY OF EUROPEAN LEGISLATION AND ITS APPLICATION

The interpretation of European legislation with a view to its application is one of the core responsibilities of the European Association's member courts. This activity puts national administrative courts in an unusual position in that, although they of course stem from the national constitutional order, they are also EU courts. Two members of the European Convention suggested that the Constitution should state that national courts are Union courts, in line with current legal opinion.[32] This suggestion was not followed up, but of course, that does not detract from the 'symbiosis between the European Court and its national counterparts'.[33]

The art of the reference for a preliminary ruling

Not all national courts take the same approach to references for preliminary rulings. The point of departure is Article 234 TEC, along with the CILFIT judgment.[34] But beyond that point, some judges may take a strict, legalistic attitude, while others may take issues into consideration that are more practical and less legalistic.[35] The preliminary rulings procedure links the work of national courts with regard to the application of EU law with that of the ECJ and

---

[32] Contribution from Alfonso Dastis and Gijs de Vries, CONTRIB 277, CONV 620/03, 13 March 2003, part 9.
[33] Weiler, op. cit., n. 6, p. 197.
[34] ECJ case 283/81, *CILFIT*, ECR 1982, p. 3415.
[35] See General Report, Chapter 2, section 2.5.

CFI (in the terminology of the Constitution for Europe, the General Court). The importance of this procedure is enormous and it is an excellent gauge of the quality of European legislation. The EC/EU legal orders and those of the Member States are becoming increasingly intertwined, a process that will inevitably continue. Their constitutional frameworks, however, are still distinct, each having its own structure, institutions and method of operation. The meshing of legal systems makes it necessary to forge links, one of which is the preliminary rulings procedure. This essential link actually dates back to the inception of the European Communities. Other links include the representation of the Member States *as such* as voting actors in the legislative process in the Council of Ministers, and the subsidiarity test that can be applied by national parliaments under the Protocol to the Constitution referred to above.

The preliminary rulings procedure is not a simple one for the referring court, the parties to the case or the ECJ. Both the referring court and the ECJ have to immerse themselves in the relationship between European legislation and the national legal system – and in such a way that the interpretation given by the Court of Justice can be of use in relation to other Member States.[36]

The long duration of the preliminary rulings procedure is cause for concern, particularly because the European Union now has 25 Member States, a substantial increase. New questions will arise concerning the implementation of European legislation in the new Member States. At the same time, the sustainability of the present institutional arrangements to keep the ECJ functioning properly will be put to the test, and ideas on changes to the procedure will be mooted. This makes prudent and selective use of the procedure by national courts all the more important. One might consider applying the CILFIT criteria in a more flexible way or referring questions to the ECJ only if it is really necessary to reach a decision on them. Another option would be to introduce some kind of filter mechanism allowing only major questions of EU law to be dealt with by the ECJ or to have national courts submit draft answers with their questions.[37]

The fact that the Councils of State and highest administrative courts can rely on preliminary rulings in their judicial work does not absolve them of the need and responsibility to be qualified and loyal interpreters of EU law themselves.[38] This is true for at least three reasons: first, because unnecessary preliminary references should be avoided; second, because appropriate use of the preliminary rulings procedure requires the ability to ask the right questions; and third, because the Councils of State in their advisory capacity cannot simply avail themselves of direct guidance from the ECJ. As the supreme administrative

---

[36] See General Report, Chapter 3, section 4.
[37] See General Report, Chapter 3, sections 4.2, 4.3 and 4.5.
[38] See General Report, Chapter 2, section 2.5.2.

courts, however, they are also obliged to hold fast to the guiding hand of the ECJ. In the light of the Köbler judgment their work has come under additional scrutiny.[39] But this does not mean that national courts are subordinate to the ECJ or that the traditional *dialogue des juges* between them has been eliminated. On the contrary, under today's circumstances, national and European judges should collaborate and communicate more with one another, showing that they are co-actors in European law.

9.   THE QUALITY OF THE INTERCONNECTIONS

This article has examined many of the interconnections in the cyclical process of the development of European law: the EU legislature, national legislatures, the ECJ, the national courts, those who prepare European policy, and national/sub-national executive authorities. Not all facets have been addressed in equal detail, and some have even gone unmentioned, such as commentary by legal practitioners and scholars. The above comments are based on pieces written for and discussed at the 2004 Colloquium of the European Association. There was consensus among the participants at that colloquium on the value of the European Association's work. One should, however, look to the future and see what can be done about the needs of the organisation's members. Many said they would welcome activities in the field of education (courses, seminars, etc.) and information management.

During the colloquium the Köbler judgment provoked much discussion. Problems are expected when a lower national court has to deal with liability incurred because the highest court breached Community law. By who, and how exactly, should such liability be determined? Can the principle of *res judicata* be abandoned? The last question was answered in the negative. Furthermore, the consequences of Köbler should be determined by national, not European, procedural law. Article 104(3) of the Rules of Procedure of the ECJ (on the simplified procedure) was believed to offer a means of reducing the Court's workload. This procedure could be combined with a 'green light' system, although in that case the ECJ would still have to take some kind of decision every time. Or it could be combined with the submission of draft answers by the referring national judge.

---

[39] ECJ case C-224/01, *Köbler*, judgment of 30 September 2003. See General Report, Chapter 2, section 3.2.

In the light of what has been said and written, a number of recommendations can be made, which can be depicted in the same setting as the European law-making cycle.[40]

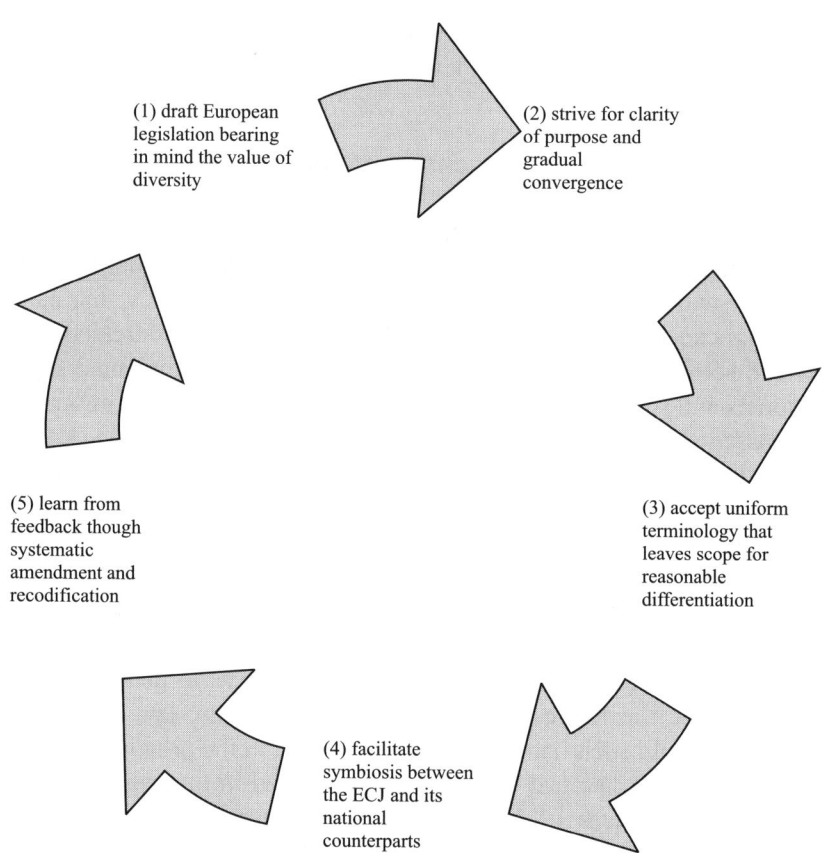

(1) draft European legislation bearing in mind the value of diversity

(2) strive for clarity of purpose and gradual convergence

(5) learn from feedback though systematic amendment and recodification

(3) accept uniform terminology that leaves scope for reasonable differentiation

(4) facilitate symbiosis between the ECJ and its national counterparts

EU law encourages and allows diversity. The first diagram, which also took a cyclical form, may have been a simplification but it clarified the links that exist. Furthermore, that diagram had no starting point, highlighting the fact that EU law is a reiterative process.

The value of diversity makes European legislation different from national legislation. Impact assessment is therefore necessary at European and national

---

[40] See p. 9

level. Differences between EU and national legislation are acceptable because the two serve different purposes.

Preliminary review should take into account the purposes of the legislation concerned. European legislation should not aim to regulate all related issues and should not become a source of confusion. In this respect, preambles and *travaux préparatoires* can be helpful, but they can also be confusing. Furthermore, clarity is not always achieved by uniformity.

Directives have been the main instruments for giving shape to the objectives of Community law. The function of national implementing legislation in the process is not to make the directive superfluous by copying it but to make national law compatible with it and achieve its aims. The question whether the terminology used in the national implementation legislation should be identical with the terminology of the directive cannot be answered in general terms.

What require further investigation are the reasons and backgrounds for the references made to the ECJ. Do the problems lie with European legislation, its implementation in national law or the activity of executive authorities? It is clear that national courts should view themselves as decentralised EU courts. In a similar sense, the ECJ is a national court. JURIFAST could develop into a very helpful tool to reduce the workload of the ECJ with regard to preliminary rulings proceedings.[41] It would make it possible to inform national judges about how other Member States approach EU law. And it would enable the art of the preliminary reference and the application of judgments to be developed further. The preliminary rulings procedure at the ECJ should leave scope for diversity.

Finally, the drafters of new European legislation should make effective use of feedback. Safeguards, such as the new role of national parliaments with regard to subsidiarity, are important but should not function as roadblocks. All this emphasises the need for all the participants in the European law-making process to work together, as co-actors.

10. PRACTISING CO-ACTORSHIP

Understanding, interpreting, implementing, applying and restating EU law – all these activities must draw on ideas and experience from both the European and

---

[41] JURIFAST is the database set up in 2004 by the Association of the Councils of State and Supreme Administrative Jurisdictions of the European Union, accessible at <http://193.191.217.21/en/jurisprudence/jurifast/jurifast_en.php> (NB: this address is expected to change in 2005-2006). The database contains judgments in which EU law is applied, either autonomously or in co-actorship with the ECJ.

the national level. In the European Union's legal order, national and European participants in law-making never operate entirely independently of each other.

The national courts play an important role as co-actors in the application of European legislation in national legal systems. The importance of this role continues to grow, as does the significance of EU law. The national courts are consequently part of the European judiciary. It is no longer possible to regard EU law as a separate area of specialisation; rather, it is an integral element of the work of any lawyer. In EU law the preliminary rulings procedure forms the link between national courts and the ECJ, which is designed to guarantee the uniform application of EU law and hence the necessary unity of law in Europe.

The legislative process in the European Union is, as far as is visible, much less based on political compromise between competing interests than are national legislative processes – although this feature is undeniably present in the lobbying activities that surround EU law-making. Instead, a defining and crucial feature of European legislation, as a product of co-actorship, is its aim of achieving a balance between the necessary unification – coordination, harmonisation or assimilation – and reasonable diversity. Feedback from the implementation, interpretation and application of EU law in national legislation and case law is one of the main sources of information for the European legislature on how best to strike this delicate balance.

Looking to the future, it is important to consider how to ensure, as far as possible, that the preliminary rulings procedure will be effective. This procedure may be regarded as the most important element of co-actorship. Apart from conceivable structural changes to the procedure, it would be useful to investigate methods that the judicial bodies themselves can adopt to make it work as well as possible. One important factor may be what approach is taken to cooperation between the national judicial bodies and the Court of Justice. Another is how policy on European law-making will develop in the coming period.

After the fifth enlargement of the EU, the time has come to shift the focus of attention from enacting entirely new legislation to codification, restatement and – where possible – simplification of the vast body of existing European legislation. Such initiatives could obtain crucial information and insights from the case law of the Member States' courts.

Finally, the Commission, the traditional initiator in EU law-making, might be invited to shift some of its attention from enacting new legislation to promoting better understanding of existing EU law and surveying its application. In this context, another question that will arise is whether soft law can continue to fill part of the role that would otherwise be played by detailed legislation in the strict sense of the word. This means that European legislation, like ECJ rulings, will have to reflect the required degree of unity and an acceptable level of diversity. In other words, EU lawmaking requires a methodology of its own, which looks ahead to implementation in national law and the activity of executive authorities. Preliminary evaluation of proposed legislation will thus assume a place of its own in the EU context; both the Commission and the Member States will have to learn to think ahead to the contributions other actors – both national and European – may make to the development of EU law.

In conclusion, each of the actors in the development of EU law can ensure that all its work will improve the quality of that law and its application, if – and only if – it makes the most of its relationships with its co-actors.

PART II

General Report.

The Quality of European Legislation and Its Implementation and Application in the National Legal Order

Linda A.J. Senden[*]

* Professor of European Law, Tilburg University, The Netherlands. The author wishes to thank Ernst Hirsch Ballin (general rapporteur), Herman Tjeenk Willink, Molle Eisma and Johan van Haersolte of the Dutch Council of State for their helpful comments and suggestions.

Chapter 1
INTRODUCTION

1.   THE APPROACH CHOSEN

The quality of European legislation has been exercising minds for some time now, within as well as outside the EU institutions. European legislation itself as well as various features of the Community system for adopting and applying European legislation have been increasingly criticised in terms of adequacy and manageability.[1] Scrutiny has increased with the ever-widening scope of European legislation. Both immigration law and criminal law, for instance, are undergoing Europeanisation. The enlargement of the European Union will also tend to exacerbate particular existing problems, such as the language regime (under the current policy the EU has twenty official languages, and probably will have more in the future, as long as the current policy is maintained) and the functioning of the system of preliminary rulings at the European Court of Justice (throughput time is already very long). Many forums are considering these issues in particular with a view to the proposed adoption of the Draft Treaty Establishing a Constitution for Europe,[2] drawn up by the European Convention. Against this background, one can understand the dedication of the 19th colloquium of the Association of Councils of State and Supreme Administrative Jurisdictions of the European Union to the theme 'The quality of European legislation and its implementation and application in the national legal orders'.

Obviously, the preparations for the colloquium and this General Report have required a further definition and delimitation of this wide-ranging theme. To this end, a discussion paper was drawn up at the beginning of 2003.[3] This paper set out the main aim of the colloquium, viz., the identification of the specific

---

[1] See, e.g., 'Rapport Public du Conseil d'Etat français. Considérations générales sur le droit communautaire', 1992, *Etudes & Documents* No. 44; the Molitor report (COM(95) 288, 21 June 1995); the Koopmans report, 1995; the Report by the Anglo-German Deregulation Group, 'Deregulation Now', 1995; and the UNICE regulatory report, 1995.

[2] CONV 850/03, 18 July 2003. The latest provisional consolidated version of the Treaty dates from 6 August 2004, CIG 87/04.

[3] Discussion paper for the meeting of the Association held in Trier on 24-25 March 2003 in preparation for the 2004 Colloquium, 'The Quality of European legislation and Its Implementation and Application in the National Legal Order', published in Newsletter 2003, No. 4, of the Association. The discussion paper can be found at <www.raadvst-consetat.be>.

E.M.H. Hirsch Ballin and L.A.J. Senden, Co-Actorship in the Development of European Law-Making
© *2005, T.M.C.ASSER PRESS, The Hague, The Netherlands and the Authors*

problems that the Association's members face – as advisors on legislation and as judicial bodies – in transposing, interpreting and applying European legislation, to analyse the causes of these problems and to take stock of possible solutions, both existing and new ones. The topic has thus been approached from the perspective of the highest judicial bodies and emphasis has been laid on those aspects of European legislation that influence its clarity and manageability in the practice of jurisdiction and of advising on legislation. In other words, the idea has not been to explore on a rather abstract level what the 'good' and 'bad' characteristics of European legislation are, but to chart on a more practical level some specific problems of that legislation and the various methods that have been devised to deal with them in the national legal orders. As such, the discussion paper addressed problems related to the European constitutional system and European legislation; national mechanisms devised to improve the quality of European legislation; problems relating to the implementation of European legislation by national parliaments; problems encountered by national courts in applying European legislation and the mechanisms devised to improve its application.

With a view to further identifying the main problems and questions which the issue of quality of European legislation poses in the Member States, a limited questionnaire was drawn up on the basis of the discussion paper and was discussed at a meeting of the national rapporteurs in Trier on 24-25 March 2003. This resulted in a more elaborate questionnaire,[4] and the national reports that were drawn up pursuant to this questionnaire form the basis of the present General Report,[5] which of course also takes account of the preparatory work. By the very nature of the subject, the questionnaire also focused on questions relating to the legislative process as such and on issues which European legislation raises for its implementation by the national legislatures. Since the Councils of State or Supreme Administrative Courts in a number of Member States only or mainly have a judicial function, it should be noted that these questions have not always been answered (e.g., Denmark) or have been answered in particular from the point of view of the national rapporteur (e.g., Austria). Apart

---

[4] See Annex 1 to this Report.

[5] Reports were submitted by the following members of the Association: Austria, Belgium, Denmark, Finland, France, Germany, Greece, Italy, Luxemburg, the Netherlands, Portugal, Spain, Sweden, and the UK. Please note that the report submitted by the British rapporteur only addresses the situation in England and Wales. Furthermore, reports were submitted by Judges Puissochet and Timmermans of the European Court of Justice and by Judge Meij of the Court of First Instance. These reports present the authors' personal views. All reports are available from the CD-Rom accompanying this volume and accessible through the website of the Association of the Councils of State and Supreme Administrative Jurisdictions, which is hosted by the Belgian Council of State <www.raadvst-consetat.be>.

from this, the General Report also builds upon a number of findings of the Helsinki colloquium of 2002, which dealt with the preliminary rulings procedure.

The next section will start with a brief reflection on the definition of quality of European legislation for the purposes of this report and, in particular, on the issues that the quality of European legislation poses for national legislatures and jurisdictions. As such, it will present the general framework for the discussion of the separate topics in Chapters 2 and 3. It will also make clear why in those Chapters of the report the emphasis is laid on 'interpretation problems' rather than on 'quality problems'. In Chapter 2, the main national findings will be presented, largely following the division into three parts of the questionnaire (though not necessarily in the order of its questions) on the causes of interpretation problems and the prevention thereof, dealing with and solving such problems and the correction of interpretation errors. In Chapter 3, the main conclusions will be presented and a number of subjects for debate and possible solutions for solving interpretation and quality problems will be put forward.

Chapters 1 and 3 have been drafted in such a way that, read in conjunction, they give an overview of the main issues the quality and interpretation of Community legislation raise for the highest national courts, while Chapter 2 gives more detailed information on the situations in the various Member States.

2.   DEFINING THE QUALITY ISSUES IN RELATION TO EUROPEAN LEGISLATION

Defining 'quality of legislation' is not an easy matter. A first observation in this respect may be that giving substance to the concept of 'quality' in relation to legislation is a highly subjective exercise: for instance, it makes a great difference whether the issue of quality of European legislation is approached from the viewpoint of the European legislature or from the perspective of a national parliament having to adopt implementing legislation or a national court having to apply it. Furthermore, evaluating legislation in terms of high or poor quality presupposes that one has a clear picture of what can or should be expected of legislation, what its purposes and functions are, what its outcome or effectiveness should be and what – drafting and democratic – standards it should meet.[6] The outcomes of such an evaluation of the national legislations of the Member States may differ, also depending on the particular aspects that receive empha-

---

[6] See also the speech delivered by H. Tjeenk Willink, Vice-President of the Dutch Council of State, at the European law conference in Stockholm, 11 June 2001. Available at <www.raadvanstate.nl>, under 'Toespraken'.

sis (for instance, more emphasis on the aim of flexibility of the law than on equality or legal certainty of the law) and the angle one takes (for instance, that of the legislature or that of the individual affected by the law). Yet, overall it can be said that such assessments will show many similarities as the framework within which legislation operates and is developed in the various national legal systems is quite comparable. Furthermore, the functions and purposes of legislation in these systems can be said to be similar as well. The case is different for European legislation.

Since the focus of the colloquium of the Association is on the quality of *European* legislation and, in particular, its consequences for the *national* legal orders, it is thus necessary to identify the issues that are at stake first. To start with, it should be understood that the issue cannot be simply approached in the same way as that of the quality of 'pure' national legislation, for only to a limited extent can the problems which present themselves in the European and the national legal orders be compared, regarding the more technical aspects of legislation, such as its complexity, transparency, vagueness, consistency, use of terminology, etc. These are problems that can be said to occur in any legal system and are therefore not specific problems of European legislation.[7] Moreover, these problems do not seem to be worse in European legislation than in national legislation.[8]

In fact, the preliminary discussions that took place within the Association have shown that the problems which European legislation poses in the national legal orders are of a more serious and structural nature and go beyond being quality problems *stricto sensu*. The picture that has emerged is not so much the problematic quality of European legislation, but rather the questions as to how European legislation is best fitted into the national legal system and how its meaning and scope have to be established in a given instance. In this light, the specific problems that European legislation[9] generates can be distinguished in problems relating, on the one hand, to the EU system as such and to the crea-

---

[7] Quite a few initiatives have been developed at the European level to improve such aspects of the quality of European legislation, including, most recently, the Interinstitutional Agreement on better law-making, concluded by the European Parliament, the Council and the Commission, OJ 2003, C 321/1. For an overview of the earlier initiatives developed in this regard by the Community institutions, see H. Xanthaki, *The Problem of Quality in EU Legislation: What on Earth is Really Wrong?*, CMLRev., Vol. 38 (2001), No. 3, pp. 653-656. See also section 3.1.3 of the discussion paper, op. cit., n. 3.

[8] See in this sense Xanthaki, op. cit., n. 7, p. 666. For an earlier more general overview of problems related to the quality of European legislation, reference may be made to A. Kellermann et al., *Improving the Quality of Legislation in Europe*, Kluwer, 1998.

[9] The emphasis here is on directives, regulations and framework decisions. For more complete references and titles of those mentioned in the report, see the national reports.

tion of legislation in that framework and, on the other, to problems of its implementation and application in the national legal orders.

Regarding the former type of problems,[10] the particular features of the European constitutional system entail that the framework and decision-making process within which European legislation is developed is very different from and,
in fact, far more complex than that of 'pure' national legislation. As a result,
European legislation has gained not only its own particular nature, but also a
purpose and function that differ from national legislation. The aims of European legislation are usually more limited in that it is geared mainly towards the
approximation of national legislation and this often still with a view to the establishment of the internal market. This affects the nature of European legislation in the sense that often it does not aim at establishing uniformity of law and
policy in the Member States and touches upon and only regulates particular
aspects of the law (for instance, tax law or environmental law), leading to pie-
cemeal legislation which is difficult to fit into the framework of existing national law. This means that European legislation leaves in fact considerable
scope for differentiation in implementation. Apart from that, European legislation triggers its own particular problems because of the lack of an explicit hierarchy of sources, its multi-language regime, the development of its proper legal
language and its high compromise level given the multiplicity of actors involved in the European decision-making process. In addition, key stages of the
decision-making process still take place behind closed doors, which can make
it even harder to trace the underlying intentions of a particular piece of legislation.

As regards the second type of problems, things obviously become even more
complicated because of the fact that European legislation has to be transposed
and applied in the national legal systems, whereas it has in fact been developed
outside those systems. In this regard, the discussion at the preparatory meeting
of the national rapporteurs in Trier made it very clear that the quality problems
which European legislation poses in the national legal orders boil down to interpretation problems, occurring both in the framework of drafting national
transposition legislation and of its application by the national courts. The later
findings of the national rapporteurs confirm the view that at the heart of these
interpretation problems lies the particular, different nature of Community legislation and the fact that the European and national legal systems still do not tie
in very well.[11] The most crucial question may therefore be how the tie-in of the
European and national legal systems can be improved and how uncertainties in

---

[10] See more in detail on this section 3 of the discussion paper, op. cit., n. 3.
[11] See Chapter 2, section 1.

the law can be removed; the answers will contribute to easier and improved transposition and application of Community legislation in the Member States. In this respect, it should also be remembered that there is an obligation on the Member States to implement and apply European legislation, but that its interpretation is ultimately to be decided by the European Court of Justice.

In dealing with the above question, there are two important limitations one should be aware of and which will even be more acute after enlargement of the EU. Firstly, given the great variety of national legal systems represented in the EU, it is inevitable that European legislation will not always be geared towards each specific national situation. Secondly, at least to a certain extent the particular features of the European legal system as described above are inherent to this system and cannot or are not likely to be changed. Consequently, European legislation will always be characterised by its particular system and terminology and it would thus be an illusion to think that it could ever be fitted smoothly into all national legal systems.[12]

Focusing then on how to deal best with the problems European legislation entails for national legislatures and courts, attention is drawn to the way in which the various actors involved in the national legislative processes respond to the obligations originating in European law, and to the way in which procedures are organised. This has triggered the following questions, which extend beyond the issue of quality of legislation in the strict sense of the word, to be dealt with in the following chapters. In particular, what different implementation techniques are used and how are the system and terminology of European legislation dealt with in implementation? What is the role of interpretation aids, such as *travaux préparatoires*, in this respect? What principles should national legislatures adopt on this? Does the way of transposition relate in any way to the number and nature of interpretation problems the national courts face? Next, when it comes to advising on legislation, what mechanisms have been devised in the Member States to improve the quality of European legislation? What *ex ante* and *ex post* examinations of European legislation take place and what is the role of the Councils of State and supreme administrative jurisdictions in this regard? What room is there for improvement?

Of course, the problem of how to deal with differences in the systems and terminologies of national and European legislations also presents itself for the national jurisdictions. What attitudes did they develop in this respect, also regarding the use of interpretation aids and other-language versions of European legislation? Furthermore, national courts face problems when transposition has

---

[12] See M. van Damme, *Naar een Europese Raad van State?*, Tijdschrift voor Bestuurswetenschappen en Publiekrecht 2001/8, p. 519, and J.P.H. Donner, *De kwaliteit van de Europese regels*, RegelMaat 2001/6, p. 216.

not taken place or only belatedly: What consequences do they attach to this in terms of direct applicability of European legislation and consistent interpretation of national law? In addition, building on the findings of the Helsinki colloquium, what other techniques and mechanisms are used or can be devised to resolve questions of interpretation and direct applicability before having recourse to the preliminary procedure, such as possible forms of informal or institutionalised cooperation between courts? What role can the Association play in this regard? Last but not least, how can it be guaranteed that in the enlarged EU the system of preliminary rulings of Article 234 EC will function as smoothly as possible? This last question is important, given the fact that it is the ECJ that ultimately decides questions of interpretation of European law, and the preliminary procedure is the most important tool for national courts to have such questions solved. In short, in the light of the developments that take place as regards the adoption of a European Constitution and the enlargement of the EU, changing the present use of Article 234 is high on the agenda.

The national responses given to the various questions raised above will be dealt with below.

Chapter 2
Interpretation of European Legislation in the Member States

As observed in Chapter 1, the problems European legislation poses in the national legal orders go beyond being mere problems of quality of this legislation. One particular point to emerge was that the problems arising within national legal systems is frequently a matter of determining the right meaning and scope of European legislation and hence of establishing the appropriate interpretation thereof. As will be seen in more detail below, the – supposedly bad – quality of European legislation is only one element which may complicate this exercise. That is also why we have chosen to take a broader angle here, focusing on 'interpretation problems' rather than mere 'quality problems'.

In this Chapter, the interpretation problems that European legislation raises in the national legal orders will first be presented and the causes thereof identified (section 1.). Next, it will be considered how and by what means the national legislatures and courts try to overcome these problems (section 2.). Finally, the consequences of interpretation errors are considered and in particular the ways to remedy these, both at the Community and the national levels (section 3.).

1. THE INTERPRETATION PROBLEMS

This first section focuses on the nature and causes of the interpretation problems as such, including those posed by the system of European legal instruments (section 1.1-1.2), and in particular on how the national legislatures are confronted and deal with these problems in their transposition of European legislation, generally (section 1.3) and more specifically as regards the Sixth Council Directive 77/388/EEC of 17 May 1977 on the harmonisation of the laws of the Member States relating to turnover taxes (*the Sixth VAT Directive*), Directive 79/409/EEC of 2 April 1979 on the conservation of wild birds (*the Bird Directive*) and Directive 92/43/EEC of 21 May 1992 on the conservation of natural habitats and of wild fauna and flora (*the Habitat Directive*) (section 1.4).

1.1 The nature and causes of interpretation problems

What kind of specific interpretation problems occur in what areas of law, both in the framework of the transposition of European legislation by the national

E.M.H. Hirsch Ballin and L.A.J. Senden, Co-Actorship in the Development of European Law-Making
© 2005, T.M.C.ASSER PRESS, *The Hague, The Netherlands and the Authors*

legislature and of its application by the national courts? To what extent are they actually attributable to the poor quality of European legislation and to what extent can other causes be identified for these interpretation problems? (questions 1.2.4 and 2.1.1 of the questionnaire)

Judges Puissochet and Timmermans of the European Court of Justice observe in their report submitted for the colloquium[13] that, in many cases, the ECJ is confronted with Community legislation whose quality leaves room for improvement and is sometimes insufficient. Yet, they also observe that the Court's experience in this respect is not representative for assessing the full scope of this problem, since the disputes submitted to it tend to relate to the most problematic cases and do not concern good legislation whose interpretation and application is not controversial. Furthermore, the fact that these cases often concern agricultural law has to do with the density of regulation in this sector. They further identify three causes for quality problems of European legislation and hence for the interpretation and application thereof. Firstly, these problems arise because the legislation undergoes many modifications without it being codified, consolidated, or regularly revised. It is thus sometimes difficult to reconstruct the text of the applicable legislation.[14] Secondly, the multiplicity of the official languages of the EU raises problems.[15] Thirdly, the legislature may omit to regulate or refrain from regulating certain modalities which are nonetheless important for a good application of the legislation at issue. This may concern, for instance, the omission to provide for transition rules in new legislation, as a result of which a legal vacuum may arise.[16]

The reports submitted by the national rapporteurs make clear that a broad range of factors causing interpretation problems of European legislation can partly be traced back to the European and partly to the national legal order. Only to a limited extent can these factors be said to concern the quality of European legislation, relating to 'technical' aspects such as the definition and use of ambiguous, complex and vague concepts and terminology, and problems of translation. Other elements which are characteristic for the European legal system and which are considered problematic are its important judge-made nature, the perceived lack of balance between case law and the general nature of the legislation, and the lack of *travaux préparatoires*. More in general, the picture

---

[13] This report was written and distributed under the responsibility of its authors.

[14] See their report for an example.

[15] See, e.g., Case C-132/99 *The Netherlands v. Commission,* ECR [2002] I-2709, paras. 25-27. See also Chapter 2, section 2.3.

[16] See, e.g., Case C-339/00 *Ireland v. Commission*, judgment of 16 October 2003, not yet reported, paras. 34-39.

that emerges from the national reports is that the main problem lies in the rather bad tie-in of and consistency among the different legal systems and the different layers of law-making. Most obviously, this concerns the European legal system *vis-à-vis* the national legal systems and cultures and vice versa, one national legal system *vis-à-vis* another, and ECJ case law and the EC Treaty *vis-à-vis* EC legislation. Yet, it is also clear that it is impossible to link up European rules perfectly with all national legal systems.

A number of state-specific factors add to the problems of implementing and interpreting European legislation, for which European legislation is not to be held responsible. These concern in particular the different levels of internal decision-making in federal or decentralised systems (**Germany, Spain**) and the fact that accession of Member States took place after European legislation was adopted (**Finland**).

Looking more closely at the latter issue, since **Finland** implemented the *acquis communautaire* in a very short period of time at the beginning of the 1990s, it is considered difficult to specify any field where there would *not* have emerged interpretation problems. Interpretation problems are actually considered to be more difficult during pre-accession implementation, as the candidate country was not involved in the decision-making process that led to the adoption of a particular European legal act. It has thus been rather difficult to implement and apply the EC Directives on bathing water, because the geographical, environmental and climatic conditions of Finland greatly differ from those of other – southern – EU countries. Most difficulties of interpretation occur in the area of indirect taxation, especially as regards VAT (see section 1.4), but also as regards agriculture, competition law, the environment and public procurement. Public procurement is an area of law which European law brought to Finland and on which very little regulation existed. So, it is not so much that difficulties of interpretation present themselves in this respect; it is rather problems of adopting a new legal framework. Interpretation problems are of a terminological nature (ambiguous terminology or legal concepts not corresponding to national terminology), of a linguistic nature because of the differences between different language versions or concern a certain imbalance between casuistry and generality in EC legislation. 'Constructive ambiguity' may even be intended, because of the lack of political will to arrive at a precise text and meaning.

The **German** legislative system is said to be characterised by four hierarchical levels: the constitutional, federal and *Länder* levels and the level of local/public law authorities. Generally speaking, European legislation is implemented at the federal, non-constitutional law level. So, the problem is not so much how to classify European law but rather how to fit it correctly into the framework of national legislation, for sometimes it is difficult to establish which is the competent level to transpose a particular issue or part thereof, of which numerous proceedings in respect of Directive 88/409/EEC testify.[17] This transposition problem may occur in every area since it is of a procedural, not a substantive nature. At the judicial level, some directives in the environmental protection area raise particular interpretation problems as they are ambiguous or even contradictory. Linguistic problems may also occur. The transposition of procedural European rules sometimes appears difficult as well.

Since **Spain** is a decentralised state in which the *Comunidades Autónomas* have their own legislative competence in the areas mentioned in Article 148 of the Constitution, the transposition of directives is rendered more complex because of the plurality of the authorities involved. There are thus numerous areas (such as health and the environment) in which the state approves framework legislation and the *Comunidades* adopt further legislation. The latter are not obliged to communicate to the Ministry of Foreign Affairs the transposition measures they adopted, with the result that the central administration cannot proceed to an effective check and cannot include these measures in the list of transposition measures communicated to the Commission. Interpretation difficulties often concern the question whether transposition legislation transposes European rules correctly or not.

The problem for the **Austrian** Administrative Court in particular concerns the question of ensuring compliance of national law with European law. Problems in the transposition of European law arise, for example, in the fields of environmental law, social law and tax law. Besides problems with respect to the Sixth VAT Directive and the Bird and Habitat Directives (see section 1.4), interpretation issues have thus arisen in the fields of agricultural market organisations[18] and state aid, and isolated problems occurred regarding residence clauses in the Trade, Commerce and Industry Regulation Act. Problems may also arise with respect to provisional court protection. These problems are traced back to the difficult access to *travaux préparatoires*, bad definitions, translation difficulties, the case law nature of European law when it comes to primary European law rules such as those on state aid and the limited amount of case law in other areas such as that of common market organisations,[19] meaning that there is no comprehensive Court clarification of questions of general interest but only a selective examination of specific problems.

---

[17] Cf., the judgment of the Federal Administrative Court of 27 April 2000, BverwG 1 C 7.99 – BverwG 111, 143.

[18] *Inter alia*, in respect of the concepts of the producer and holdings in Regulation 3950/92/ EEC of 28 December 1992 establishing an additional levy in the milk and milk products sector or other provisions, OJ 1992, L 405/1. See also section 1.2.1 and n. 33.

[19] Cf., Case C-268/01 *Agrargenossenschaft Alkersleben,* ECR [2003] I-4353.

The **Dutch** report points to the substantive fine-tuning of secondary European rules with the EC Treaty and of secondary rules among themselves as being problematic. Yet, this problem also arises in relation to national legislation. The more specific legislation is and the more it is embedded in a systematic whole, the smaller the interpretation problems become. Examples of this are customs law and pharmaceutical legislation. The more general legislation is and the more loose ends it contains, the more questions are likely to arise regarding its scope, the possibilities for additional national policy, etc. Examples of this are environmental law and energy law.

The **Italian** rapporteur observes that interpretation difficulties are often similar to those occurring in the internal legal order, such as whether a legal rule has a specialised nature that prohibits its amendment by a later general rule.[20] Particular interpretation problems have occurred, however, in the area of public procurement as regards abnormally low tenders. This concerns the interpretation of Article 21, paragraph 1 bis of Law No. 109 of 11 February 1994 implementing Article 30 of Directive 93/37/EEC of 14 June 1993 concerning the coordination of procedures for the award of public works contracts.[21] On the basis of this Law, abnormally low tenders are easier to establish – and thus to exclude – than on the basis of the directive as interpreted by the ECJ. The reasons for this somewhat divergent transposition are said to lie in the traditional suspicion of the Italian legal order about too low price offers and in the tradition of pre-eminence of the administration.

The **Portuguese** rapporteur mentions the articulation and harmonisation of two legal systems that have to be applied simultaneously as a source of interpretation and application difficulties. In particular Regulation 2950/83 concerning professional training in the framework of the ESF has given rise to such problems, as regards the settlement of the final payments for the initiators of training activities. In the end, the ECJ established that the final decision on this lies with the Commission and that a national administration can only take immediate, provisional measures with a view to preventing irreparable damage. As a result, national courts have had to declare the national decisions and reimbursement orders void. So, it is foremost the relation between a European regulation and national implementing regulations and their coordinated interpretation and application that caused problems.

In the **Greek** report, three main reasons are given for the interpretation difficulties: (a) the quality and peculiarity of European legislation, (b) the differences between the systems and terminologies of national law and European

---

[20] Cf., Council of State, 4th Section, No. 1313 of 11 March 2003.
[21] OJ 1993, L 199/54.

law, in particular in the case that the area concerned was already the object of detailed and complex national regulation, whose characteristics have not been taken sufficiently into account in the adoption of the European legislation and (c) the conflicts between national interests or the interests of certain social or professional categories and European interests, in particular in cases where no clearly articulated compromises were reached on these conflicts. The transposition and application of the directives on the mutual recognition of diplomas (in particular Directive 89/48/EEC) provides a good illustration of these difficulties because of the peculiarities of the Greek constitutional regime of higher education.

From the perspective of the courts, the **British** rapporteur also states that three types of problems come to mind. The first type concerns the application of a particular form of words to a particular factual situation. For example: Does car hire fall within the 'transport services' exemption from the consumer protection requirements of Directive 97/7/EC on the protection of consumers in respect of distance contracts?[22] Or: When are two medicines 'essentially similar' for the purposes of the abridged authorisation procedure now contained in Directive 2001/83 on the Community code relating to medicinal products for human use?[23] Such problems are considered standard in any legal system, and are accentuated by the nature of the Community legislative process and by the need to phrase Community instruments in terms that can be given a meaning in all national legal systems and that may therefore be less precise than those used in national legislation. Whilst problems of this kind can to some extent be reduced by detailed definition clauses, or by a drafting technique which seeks to provide for all eventualities, such techniques can themselves cause problems when a purportedly exhaustive list or definition becomes out-of-date. The second type of problem is caused by (or is at least rendered less easily soluble by) the existence of a different meaning in the different language versions of the directive.[24] The British rapporteur suspects that such ambiguities are difficult to avoid. The third type of problem is uncertainty concerning the legal consequences that are intended to follow from a Community instrument. To take four examples that have recently been litigated in the UK: 1) Do provisions of a directive have direct effect in given circumstances?; 2) Is it intended that a fail-

---

[22] OJ 1997, L 144/19. This question was referred by the High Court. See Case C-336/03 *Easy-Car*, still pending.

[23] OJ 2001, L 311/67. This question has been the subject of three references from the UK and one from Denmark: C-368/96 *Generics (UK) and others,* ECR [1998] I-796; C-106/01 *Novartis Pharmaceuticals,* ECR [2004], judgment of 29 April 2004, not yet reported; C-36/03 *Approved Prescription Services*, still pending;C-74/03 *Smith Kline Beecham*, still pending.

[24] See, e.g., Case C-372/88 *MMB v. Cricket St Thomas,* ECR [1990] I-1345 and Case C-296/95 *R v. CCE ex parte EMU Tabac,* ECR [1998] I-1605. See further also section 1.4.1.

ure to regulate a bank in accordance with the standards required by a directive, or a failure to ensure particular standards of environmental protection, should give rise to a remedy in damages?; 3) Is it legitimate to implement an apparently absolute obligation to achieve animal health by a provision which requires all reasonable endeavours to be taken, and imposes penal sanctions if they are not?; 4) Is an excise duty directive intended to regulate the incidence of the burden of proof in national enforcement proceedings? The rapporteur considers it unrealistic to suggest that the Community legislature, operating under the inevitable constraints of a political process, should seek to anticipate and answer all such questions in the text of the instrument. However, where there is the necessary consensus that certain legal consequences should follow from an instrument, there may be scope for saying so. The problems are either resolved by the English courts themselves or are referred to the ECJ.

The **Belgian** rapporteur gives numerous examples of interpretation difficulties of European legislation that may occur in a national legal order,[25] relating for instance to the exact scope of certain European law notions and the binding nature of certain aspects of directives. Yet, he concludes that these do not seem to be of a fundamental nature, at least not different from the interpretation difficulties one comes across in the development of any other legal order. These difficulties may even be considered relatively marginal, given the complexity and technicality of European law and the number of players that are involved in its drafting. Some problems go, however, beyond simple interpretation problems and concern frictions between European legislation and constitutional requirements. The Belgian report gives examples of this, which relate, *inter alia*, to the obligation contained in some directives to enable control of the legality of administrative acts adopted in the application of national transposition measures before independent instances; the retroactivity of national transposition legislation which may be imposed in the case of belated implementation; and the allocation in some directives of certain types of proceedings to a non-judicial body (such as concerning the execution of contracts),[26] which is prohibited under Article 144 of the Belgian Constitution. The legislation department of the Council of State may give advice on how to reconcile the secondary European law provisions and constitutional requirements and other provisions on funda-

---

[25] Relating to different European law provisions in the area of immigration and free movement of persons, Directive 75/442/EEC, Directive 76/160/EEC, Directive 76/464/EEC, Directive 81/851/EEC, Directive 85/203/EEC, Directive 85/337/EEC, Directive 89/105/EEC, Directive 89/552/EEC, Directive 91/263/EEC, Directive 90/388/EEC, Regulation 2081/92, Directive 92/96/EEC, Directive 95/26/EC, Decision 96/449/EC, Directive 97/33/EC, Directive 2001/20/EC, Directive 2001/42/EC and Directive 2001/55/EC.

[26] Cf., Art. 8(1) of Directive 92/44/EEC.

mental rights.[27] The Court of Arbitration also keenly watches this process as regards the maintenance of respect for constitutional provisions in the framework of transposing a directive.[28]

The **French** rapporteur observes that, at the stage of transposition, interpretation difficulties may occur as a result of the fact that the scope of particular provisions has been underestimated at the time of their negotiation or because the compromise that has been achieved in the framework of the co-decision procedure goes beyond the initial objectives of a provision. Problems may also occur in respect of the transposition of very specified notions. Apart from that, the present system of drafting European legislation is not considered to suffer very much from a lack of transparency, but more from the difficulty to reconcile, within one single text, the different national legal traditions, which affects the clarity of the rules. A complication is how to express in all official EU languages one and the same legal concept.

The **Swedish** rapporteur does not see any particular interpretation problems and considers that the interpretation and application of European law is by now an everyday affair and that the courts can often solve the problems themselves.

1.2   The new hierarchy and typology of European legal instruments

To what extent are interpretation problems attributable to the current system of European legal instruments and the lack of a clear hierarchy of European norms? Will the new typology of European legal acts, proposed in Article I-32 of the Draft Treaty Establishing a Constitution for Europe (hence: Draft Constitutional Treaty), facilitate the interpretation and application of European law? Will the differentiation of European legal instruments create new legal problems (e.g., the use of the open method of coordination)? (questions 1.1.1-1.1.4 of the questionnaire)

Overall, the national reports show that the lack of an explicit hierarchy of sources in EC law is not perceived as very problematic and does not appear to have posed particular problems for the interpretation and application of European law by national courts. In view of this, it may not come as a surprise that the national rapporteurs do not express high expectations as regards the changes the Draft Constitutional Treaty proposes to the current system of legal instruments. Moreover, a number of flaws in this new typology of acts are mentioned.

---

[27] See, for instance, its Advice 33.409 of 26 June 2002.
[28] Cf., C.A., 118/2003, 17 September 2003.

Judges Puissochet and Timmermans also observe that the lack of clarity on the hierarchy of Community norms seems to constitute only a minor problem that has not yet given rise to any fundamental judgments. They discuss three cases which touched upon this issue in some form or another, but which did not in fact require the Court to rule on this aspect.[29]

1.2.1 *Problems connected to the present system of European legal instruments*

As regards the issue of the hierarchy of European norms, the **Swedish** rapporteur observes that the lack of clarity only concerns the different forms of secondary legislation, which seldom raised problems for the Swedish legislature and courts. If a conflict between European norms arises, it has to be solved in the same way as in the case of national norms that are incompatible. The **Danish** rapporteur sees no specific problems regarding the present level of clarity on the hierarchy of European legal norms. The distinction between binding and non-binding instruments is kept in mind when applying non-standard legal instruments such as resolutions. The **Finnish** rapporteur is not aware of any major problems in this respect either, stating further that the principle of supremacy of European law obliges the legislature to implement any European legal act requiring national legislative measures regardless of its position in the hierarchy of European law.[30] In **Germany** no specific problems regarding the hierarchy issue occurred; most interpretation and application problems have a national cause (see section 1.1). In **Portugal**, the principle of the primacy of European law directs legislative activity as well as its application, without its hierarchy posing any specific problems in this regard. The practice of the **Belgian** Council of State does not reveal any particular difficulties with the lack of clarity concerning the hierarchy of European legal instruments either. It is thus considered easy to establish whether a regulation or directive implements another one or not. The **British** rapporteur also states that the fact that, in the present system, no distinction is made between legislative and implementing instruments does not pose significant problems for the courts. Since the adopting body is always mentioned in the title of the instrument, it is not considered difficult to identify the power under which the instrument was adopted.

The **Spanish** rapporteur also thinks the difficulties that are expressed as regards the existing system of secondary legal instruments are rather theoretical

---

[29] Case C-136/96 *Scotch Whisky Association,* ECR [1998] I-4571 (which was solved by having recourse to the adage of *lex specialis* and *lex generalis*); Case C-25/02 *Rinke,* ECR [2003] I-8349; Case C-133/99 *The Netherlands v. Commission,* ECR [2002] I-4943, paras. 18-33.

[30] See, for example, the decision of the Supreme Administrative Court in the *Chiquita Finland* Case, KHO 1996, A 30.

than real. Although there is undeniably a blurring of the distinction between regulations and directives and a lack of distinction between fundamental and implementing legislation, these circumstances have not complicated the application of European norms. Furthermore, second and third-pillar instruments in practice did not produce the problems dreaded, as two Supreme Court decisions show that it is aware of the kind of instruments it is dealing with and how it is to understand their legal status.[31] The **Greek** rapporteur considers the distinction between primary and secondary European law to be similar to the national distinction familiar to the national judge, i.e., between the Constitution and laws, and in practice a distinction reveals itself between framework regulations and implementing ones. The **French** rapporteur states that the problems which France faces in the transposition of directives rather concern problems of French administrative organisation to deal with the number of directives and their appropriateness than their interpretation or lack of clarity regarding their hierarchical position. It is rather the objectives of directives that need clarification than the legal nature of the texts themselves.

Nonetheless, the **French** rapporteur also observes that in a number of cases the absence of a hierarchy of European norms entailed difficulties within the French legal order. For the legislature, the fact that no distinction is made between the legislative and the implementation levels makes it difficult to assess what acts actually have to be submitted to parliament and what the position of parliament is in implementation. Parliament has criticised the detailedness of directives, but the main problem is the huge number of directives that have to be transposed. As regards the Council of State, the government has assigned it the task of sorting out which proposals for European acts, according to national law, touch upon the competence of parliament and which do not. The Council of State developed the principle that European legislative acts must be understood to be those legal acts that in France have to be regulated by laws. The nature of the transposition act depends on the legislative or implementing nature of a directive, depending on its contents.[32] At the level of jurisdiction, problems may occur as regards the application of European law[33] and the direct effect of European rules. In particular, the lack of clarity concerning the nature of European acts prevents the national courts from relying on their designation

---

[31] Tribunal Supremo, judgment of 8 July 2002, concerning in particular Council Framework Decision of 28 May 2001 (2001/413/JHA) combating fraud and counterfeiting of non-cash means of payment; Tribunal Supremo, judgment of 14 June 2002, concerning the Council Common Position of 27 December 2001 on the application of specific measures to combat terrorism.

[32] Conclusions of commissioner of the government Lamy, 3 December 1999, *Association ornithologique et mammalogique de Saône et Loire*, No. 164789, p. 380.

[33] See the conclusions of commissioner of the government Séners, 11 July 2001, *FNSEA et autres*, No. 219494 et seq., p. 340.

for determining their direct applicability or not. A more in-depth examination of the nature of the legal act at issue is called for in this respect.

In **Italy**, the lack of clarity concerning the hierarchy of European sources raises difficulties both as regards the interpretation of similar though not identical norms contained in European law rules of a different level and as regards the direct effect of European rules in the national legal order. According to the **Austrian** rapporteur, the absence of a hierarchy of sources does not raise specific problems and the problem of a hierarchy of norms will persist, no matter how sophisticated or 'simple' the hierarchical structure of the legal system will be. Many questions that now arise are considered to result rather from the relation of norms regulating different fields of European law than from their hierarchy. In this respect, mention is made of the regulation of the common market organisation and the state aid rules, in the framework of which the relation between primary and secondary law, however, also arises.[34] The occasional cases in which the hierarchy of European norms caused problems on the judicial level in **the Netherlands** relate to Regulation 259/93 on the supervision and control of shipments of waste within, into and out of the European Union and the various general and specific waste directives. This has led to preliminary questions.[35] Problems have also occurred as regards Directive 76/464/EEC on pollution caused by certain dangerous substances discharged into the aquatic environment of the Community.

1.2.2 *Introduction of a new hierarchy of norms and typology of legal acts*

Articles I-33 to I-37 of the Constitutional Treaty, reproduced in Annex II to this report, introduce a new hierarchy of norms by establishing a number of new legal acts of the Union, replacing as such those listed in the present Article 249 EC. These new legal acts comprise in particular the European law, the European framework law, the European regulation, and the European decision. This new categorisation entails also a distinction between legislative and non-legislative acts, delegated regulations, and implementing acts.

Introducing an explicit hierarchy of norms in European law is welcomed for a variety of reasons such as clarity, simplicity and certainty and its possible contribution to the facilitation and improvement of the transposition and application of EU law in the national legal orders (**Sweden**, **Italy**, **the Netherlands**,

---

[34] See the judgment of the Administrative Court of 20 March 2003, 2000/17/0084, where the question of the relation between the common market organisation of beef and the EC state aid rules arose.

[35] Cases C-307-311/00 *Oliehandel Koeweit BV and others,* Order of 27 February 2003, ECR [2003] I-1821.

Finland, Germany, Portugal, Belgium). The **British** rapporteur welcomes it from the point of view of public and judicial understanding of Community legislative procedures. Furthermore, it is also considered that the binding or non-binding status of any new form of legal instruments is made clear (**Denmark**). The proposals contained in the Draft Constitutional Treaty may also be favourable to the division of work within the European institutions (**Germany**) and lead to stronger focus of the European Parliament on the legal preparation of legislation (**Belgium**). Furthermore, they may help to make the European citizen understand better the mechanism of EU legislation. Unification of all pillar instruments and the distinction between legislative, implementing and delegated instruments are also seen as advantages (**Spain, Belgium**) as well as the exclusion of the use of atypical instruments when legislative acts are in the pipeline (**Spain**). The proposals were also welcomed in the **Finnish** Government Report to Parliament of 2 September 2003,[36] which was shared by the Grand Committee opinion and the Foreign Affairs Committee.[37] The proposals are seen as a possibility to restrict EU legislation to the most important and general issues and to leave the technical details of regulation to be decided by the Commission.

At the same time, however, a number of drawbacks of the new typology of acts have been mentioned as well. Thus, the **Spanish** rapporteur thinks that framework laws may still be drawn up in a very detailed way, leaving virtually no room to manoeuvre to the Member States and that it is strange that the instrument of regulation is used for both delegated and implementing acts. The **Belgian** rapporteur also regrets that no clear criterion has been introduced to distinguish between legislative and implementing acts. Furthermore, the fact that future 'regulation' will be of a very different nature than 'regulation' at present adds to the confusion. The **British** rapporteur observes that some aspects of the proposed changes, e.g., the notion of 'implementing powers' in Article I-37, does not seem entirely clear. The **Swedish** rapporteur considers the language used in Article I-33 to be more confusing than enlightening and the distinction between legislative and non-legislative normative acts serving no purpose. In the **Dutch** report, it is considered problematic that the scope of legislation has not been substantively defined, especially since the relationship between delegated legislative powers and implementing competences is not clearly explained. It is also wondered how European laws and framework laws – as legislative acts – can be adopted in those areas in which the Treaty explicitly excludes harmonisation of national legislation. As such, the new typology

---

[36] VNS 2/2003 vp.
[37] SuVL 2/2003 vp and UaVM 4/2003 vp, respectively.

will not solve the questions surrounding the substantive consistency of European acts. The **Italian** rapporteur finds that the new typology proposes to specify the status of each European act in the national legal order, yet without specifying explicitly whether framework laws have direct effect and, if so, what the scope of that direct effect is.

The **Austrian** rapporteur doubts whether greater clarity can be achieved in this respect at all[38] and whether the proposed reduction in instruments will lead to a reduction in interpretation problems. He considers in particular that the question whether a specific norm is in line with primary law may always arise, no matter how many layers a hierarchically structured system may have. The proposed system is considered fairly close to the system in **Greece**, where many questions and case law have arisen regarding the application of the constitutional rules on legislative delegation. It is thus expected that the new classification of European acts and the separation which is made between legislative and implementing power will also be at the origin of new interpretation questions, at least initially, with respect to the definition of the essential and non-essential elements of the law and framework law; the check of the contents of delegated regulations in relation to aims of the law and the framework law; and the distinction between delegated regulations and implementing regulations. The **German** rapporteur also considers that the proposed model largely corresponds to the German system, which distinguishes between laws, framework laws and regulations. However, it will of course not solve the interpretation problems relating to the German federal legal system, as was discussed in section 1.1. The **French** rapporteur observes that the proposed reform in essence boils down to a change in terminology, without modifying the nature or the adoption procedure of legal acts. Furthermore, no substantive criterion for classifying the various acts has been proposed. In view of this, he judges it preferable to maintain the specificity of the Community system and not to try to synthesise the various national systems, which do not distinguish between legislative and implementing areas in the same way.

1.2.3 *Problems connected to the use of other instruments*

Even though Article I-33 aims at reducing the number of European legal instruments, it is clear at the same time that the Constitutional Treaty allows for a certain differentiation of European instruments (as does the present EC Treaty), involving in particular the use of the open method of coordination (OMC),

---

[38] In this respect it is also referred to the Lamfalussy report; Final Report of the Committee of Wise Men on the Regulation of European Securities Markets, Brussels, 15 February 2001.

self-regulatory instruments such as collective agreements[39] and soft law instruments. One may therefore wonder about the consequences this use has for the correct interpretation and application of European law. Only rather exceptionally, the use of such other instruments is rejected (**Finland**), but a number of rapporteurs raise the point of clarification of their legal status.

Some rapporteurs do not see what problems this use could create (**Sweden**) or in what respect these problems might differ from those occurring already (**Austria**). The **French** rapporteur also thinks that OMC, applicable only in areas outside EU competence and based on the idea of peer pressure, affects the national legal orders only in a very limited way. Self-regulation and co-regulation are considered to have a more direct influence and to be closer to a number of national legal systems. Even though they may entail the establishment of rules or informal rules that may be easier to apply because they are more in tune with day-to-day practice, they do not contribute to a more coherent, transparent, democratic and simplified system of Community legal instruments.

Others have declared themselves rather in favour of the use of such instruments. The **Italian** rapporteur thus finds that OMC, co-regulation and self-regulation all boil down to the use of soft law instruments, which facilitate the achievement of consensus, express some sensibility in areas in which more binding rules cannot be established and testify of a search for consensus and legitimacy with a particular category of persons. OMC is considered a harmonisation instrument which may bring the national legal orders of the Member States closer together in areas outside EU competence. However, the non-legally binding status and functions of these instruments should be clarified. The **German** rapporteur finds that the use of OMC outside the Union's competences does not pose legal problems as long as no strict obligations are imposed. Self-regulation and co-regulation are considered to have political advantages, but they may also create situations that lack clarity and create lacunae in the regulation when they do not have a strict legal effect. The **Greek** rapporteur sees advantages of the use of OMC, but is also of the opinion that its use should not be generalised, given that it does not have legally binding force. The use of collective agreements is considered legitimate, as they constitute a method which conforms to national tradition[40] and plays its role in an area in respect of which the EU has to take national diversities into account. New interpretation and application problems may occur in respect of soft law instruments since the use of such instruments is not common administrative

---

[39] See, *inter alia*, Arts. II-88 and III-212 of the Constitutional Treaty.
[40] E.g., Art. 22 of the Greek Constitution.

practice in Greece. Therefore, they should be demystified and their advantages and disadvantages should be considered before using them. More in general, recourse to instruments that depart from traditional unilateral law-making presupposes the clarification and consolidation of general principles of European law as well as the development of mechanisms for ensuring the conformity of new methods with these principles. The **Portuguese** rapporteur is of the opinion that OMC should be introduced into the Treaty with a view to framing these policies into the European legal system and that it could have a more useful and effective application in the Member States if it had an obligatory nature in a number of previously defined areas. Self-regulation and co-regulation are deemed adequate – though limited – means of regulation in economic and social sectors involving a European embedding. Co-regulation in particular enables cooperation between sectors interested and the European institutions, which may lead to the adoption of a European legislative act laying down the objectives to be realised by the parties concerned.

Both the **Finnish** government and parliament have taken rather negative standpoints concerning OMC as a regulatory method, expressing the fear that the use thereof may lead to unintended expansion of EU competences and confusion as to the limits of the powers of the EU institutions. The use of collective agreements by management and labour has been actively supported. Yet, attention is also drawn to the fact that self-regulation and co-regulation without a clear constitutional or legislative framework could create specific problems, both as sources of European obligations of the Member States and as means for creating and ensuring European rights of individuals in the national legal systems. The **Belgian** rapporteur also thinks that the use of methods such as OMC may produce interpretation and implementation difficulties in the Member States, whenever this entails the use of instruments that fit in better with the Community method, such as framework directives. Such a use cannot be excluded since it is thought that OMC may also be applied in areas in which the EU has competence. The Belgian rapporteur further considers the unclear legal status of 'guidelines' as well as the fact that the use of such instruments escapes the judicial control of the ECJ to be problematic. The **Dutch** rapporteur, too, regards the proliferation of policy instruments with an obscure legal status as problematic. Even though they play a role particularly in the process of national policy development and legislation and in the framework of the evaluation of the effectiveness and opportuneness of proposed policy and legislation, it is also clear that they do not have a direct legal impact in the national legal order. On a case-by-case basis, it will have to be considered what significance to attribute to these instruments both from a legal and from a policy point of view.

1.3   Implementation techniques: the relation between transposition and application

How is European legislation implemented in the national legal order? What are the transposition methods or implementation techniques most frequently used? How does the way of implementation by the national legislature affect the application of European law by the national courts: do some transposition methods entail more/less interpretation problems than others? (questions 1.2.1 – 1.2.3 of the questionnaire)

1.3.1 *General observations*

It appears that national practices vary to quite some extent when it comes to choosing the way of implementing European legislation. Thus, literal transposition may be very common in one Member State (**Italy**) and hardly ever considered an appropriate solution in another (**Germany**). Some rapporteurs state that it is difficult or even impossible to categorically choose for one or the other transposition method and to express a preference for full alignment of the national legal system with the European system or merely for an *ad hoc* adaptation. There is not one general technique for solving the problems that arise; this may depend, *inter alia*, on the subject at issue (**Austria**), the general need for modernising legislation and the extent of the reform required (**Sweden**). Furthermore, adapting the entire national legal system in a particular area is not always possible, even if perhaps deemed preferable, because deadlines are too short for doing so (**Germany, Finland, the Netherlands, Sweden**).

The recourse to methods of accelerated transposition, including transposition by referral and by delegation, also varies quite considerably from one Member State to another. In particular transposition by referral – meaning that EC provisions are not implemented literally; the national legislation merely refers to these provisions – is not applied at all in some Member States (**Italy, Portugal, Greece**), rarely in other states (**Germany**) and increasingly in yet other states, even if only under certain conditions (**the Netherlands, Finland, France, the UK**). Its less labour-intensive and time-consuming nature is seen as advantages of this method (**the Netherlands**). Its flaws are considered to be the partial lack of parliamentary supervision, disrupting the coherence of the national system, and less transparency of the national legal system (**the Netherlands, Finland**). Transposition by delegation concerns the empowerment of a lower rule-maker, for example a Minister, to take the necessary transposition measures by means of lower rules. Most Member States seem to allow this, under the same conditions as apply to 'pure' national legislation. More generally, transposition takes place at the same level as prescribed or chosen for the adoption of 'pure' national legislation in a particular area and according to the same rules or conditions (cf., **Sweden**, **Germany**).

Opinions seem to differ as to what the correlation is between the method of transposition or implementation technique chosen and the subsequent interpretation and application problems of European and transposition legislation that national courts are confronted with. Thus, the **Luxemburg** and **Austrian** rapporteurs think that the transposition method does not matter and that none of the transposition methods can avoid problems in the administration of justice. The national courts will have to try to solve these problems by relying on the direct effect of European legislation and by way of consistent interpretation. The **Austrian** Administrative Court thus had to reverse a number of decisions by public authorities, as a result of the fact that the Law on Foodstuffs, which partly transposed Directive 79/112/EEC on the approximation of the laws of the Member States relating to the labelling, presentation and advertising of foodstuffs for sale to the ultimate consumer,[41] had not done so properly, as preliminary rulings of the ECJ made clear.[42] But also if an entire national legal system has been changed – which may occur in particular with a view to the application of European regulations – interpretation problems often arise. For example, the direct application of Article 9 of Commission Regulation 3887/92, laying down detailed rules for applying the integrated administration and control system for certain European aid schemes, entailed interpretation problems because of its ambiguity; problems the Administrative Court managed to resolve itself. The **British** rapporteur observes that judges have occasionally suggested, where the copy-out method of implementation was not used, that it might have been simpler to use it.

1.3.2 *National approaches*

In **Austria**, no preference is expressed for full or only partly alignment of the national legal system in implementation. This depends on the area at issue and the differences between existing legislation and European legislation (see also section 1.4 on the implementation of the Sixth VAT Directive). Problems arise both when the entire system of a directive is taken over in national legislation and when only adaptations are made. In some cases implementation can be carried out by means of regulations of the administration, for instance as regards the common organisation of the market of agricultural products. But there are constitutional restrictions to this method, as there is a strict principle of

---

[41] OJ 1979, L 33/1.
[42] Joined cases C-421/00, C-426/00 and C-16/01 *Sterbenz and Haug,* ECR [2003] I-1065.

legality in the Federal Constitution.[43] The Austrian rapporteur further considers that the national court must always examine whether the national rule is in compliance with European law, no matter whether the national law uses the terms of a directive or not. Therefore, interpretation problems will normally not depend on the method of transposition chosen. It is thus not considered to matter whether the national legislation states 'bank' or 'credit institute' when implementing an EU norm that mentions 'banks' or 'credit institutes'. What counts is that each body affected by the European law provision is also covered by the national provision. Interpretation problems may arise with respect to the concept of 'bank' as well as with respect to the concept of 'credit institute' even if the same expression is used as in the European provision.

In **Finland**, the basic rule is that the terms used in European legislation should also be adopted for national legislation. Where national terminology differs from European terminology, it must be assessed on a case-by-case basis whether to retain or to alter the national terminology. Clear legal language and a correct and effective transposition of European legislation may sometimes require additional explanation or specification of the directive concerned in the national legislation. The three main forms of implementing directives in Finland are rewriting, incorporation and referral. Rewriting national legislation so that it complies with the requirements of the directive can be considered the standard method of transposition. Total or partial incorporation concerns the direct insertion of the text of a directive into national law, which is advisable in the case a directive is very detailed or contains technical specifications and the Member State has little or no latitude in its implementation. This method makes it easier to ensure a clear complex of rules, in which the directive and the national law are integrated in a smooth and coherent way. The referral method should only be used in cases where the text of the directive is specific or technical, again not leaving latitude in implementation, and where the other methods for some reason are difficult to use.[44] The delegation of legislative competence is possible on the same conditions that normally govern delegation pursuant to the Constitution, which excludes implementation of more signifi-

---

[43] Cf., Constitutional Court, 6 June 1998, V 6/98, V 7/98 and V 8/98, CCR 15.189/1998. In contrast to Öhlinger, 'Legalitätsprinzip und Europäische Integration', in: Österreichische Parlamentarische Gesellschaft – Austrian Parliamentary Society (eds.), *75 Jahre Bundesverfassung*, 1995, p. 645, the Constitutional Court held that it is necessary to have a determinate basis in an Act of Parliament, even when there is a directive the contents of which are to be transposed into domestic law.

[44] In so observing, the Finnish rapporteur shares the views expressed in the Legal Draftsman's Guide to the European Union – Guidelines for Drafting National Legislation; originally adopted in 1996, available in English since 1997 and drawn up by the Finnish Ministry of Foreign Affairs, Unit of Action Plan for Central and Eastern Europe, pp. 34-35.

cant legal issues by delegation. If the matter at issue requires an Act of Parliament, this also goes for the implementation of directives in this area. Quantitatively, a huge amount of European legislation was implemented by making combined use of the delegation and referral or incorporation methods. This use was inspired by the need to implement the 'old approach' technical barriers to trade directives, which rather resemble technical standards than legal provisions. The same applies to technical rules in areas such as the environment and agriculture.

In its legislation advisory function, the **Dutch** Council of State takes as a point of departure that in implementation the terminology and system of European legislation should be maintained as far as possible, especially when it covers the basic characteristics of a regulatory system. Examples of this are VAT, environmental law and intellectual property. Since this approach may be problematic when the European and Dutch terminologies and systems differ and European legislation only covers a small part of the national system (and adapting the entire national system to the European system may not be desirable or feasible), the system of the directive will then be adopted for only part of the legislative complex or the directive provisions will be inserted in the national system. This approach was adopted for the transposition of the Merger Directive, which covers only a particular aspect of corporate tax law. Yet, sticking to the national system and terminology may lead to ever-increasing discrepancies between the national and European systems, if European legislation is adopted which builds upon previous legislation. This has occurred in environmental law, legislation on pharmaceuticals, equal treatment legislation and as regards VAT. In more recent years, the transposition methods of referral and delegation have often been used. Referral may be static, meaning that reference is made exclusively to existing European rules,[45] or dynamic, meaning reference is made to European rules including future changes.[46] The Council of State does not reject this, but has stipulated a number of conditions for the use of the referral method: provisions regarding entry into force have to be adopted, the legislation is to concern subjects in respect of which no choices can be made or no discretion is left as to its implementation (technical annexes), referral provisions must be specified and they must be published in the *Staatscourant*. Transposition by delegation also occurs with some regularity, and the

---

[45] E.g., Art. 1, para. 1 and Art. 3 of the *Warenwetbesluit etikettering van schoeisel*.

[46] E.g., Art. 4, para. 1/2 of the *Besluit fysieke belasting*, which relates to Council Directive 90/269/EEC of 29 May 1990 on the minimum health and safety requirements for the manual handling of loads where there is a risk particularly of back injury to workers. Amendments have to be published in the Dutch *Staatscourant*, making mention of the date as from which they have to be observed.

Council of State has no objections to this either as long as the legislation concerns technical implementation matters. In other cases, however, it is considered to go against the primacy of the legislature and to erode the position of parliament. The Council rejects the creation of the possibility of deviating from the law by lower rules. There is no unanimity on these points of departure; the government has a stronger preference for the use of accelerated implementation methods, which leads to discussions with the Council of State and with parliament.[47]

The technical assistance staff of the **Portuguese** Supreme Administrative Court, which has no legislation advisory function, established that in the case of technical matters there is a consistent practice of copying the system and contents of the European rules completely. In the case of issues that were already regulated by law in some way before the adoption of European rules or that are considered to have an impact that goes beyond a limited or technical sector, the tendency is to transpose European legislation by introducing national regulation that has its own system and rules, or the occasion is seized to reformulate the national legislation significantly. In the case of directives of a more frequent application and a higher social impact, transposition implies the establishment of a new systematised body of regulation in which the European law changes required are introduced, while maintaining the national rules that are deemed compatible with European law. An illustration of this is the transposition of Directive 2001/17/EC on the reorganisation and winding-up of insurance undertakings. The Portuguese rapporteur thinks that this way of transposing contributes to clarity and legal certainty, as maintaining the former national rules with some amendments would have raised more doubts and interpretation difficulties. Sometimes transposition measures are not deemed necessary, either because the existing national legislation already guarantees the aims of the directive or because the directive exclusively establishes obligations for the Member States as regards the EU. Its implementation then flows from regular administrative action or from the relations of state bodies with the EU. Yet, this entails the risk of having ill-founded confidence in the existing internal legal instruments for guaranteeing the objectives of directives. This was established in relation to Council Directive 89/665/EEC, concerning the application of review procedures to the award of public supply and public works contracts, which was not implemented in time and in respect of which it was held that specific transposition measures were not necessary. In the end, however, the Portuguese government admitted the necessity to adopt legislation in order to

---

[47] E.g., the proposal to amend the General Equal Treatment Act and some other laws with a view to implementing Directives 2000/43/EC and 2000/78/EC; *Kamerstukken II* 2002/03, 28 770.

ensure the availability of procedural means to guarantee the effect of definite, posterior decisions of administrative tribunals. It is further observed that national jurisdictions, albeit wrongly, often have a different attitude towards directly applicable European legislation and national transposition legislation; the tendency is to interpret the latter rather as 'pure' national texts, whereas the former are interpreted in the light of the European law objectives to be achieved. The more transposition boils down to a reformulation of rules, the more national law concepts will be adhered to and the more orientation will be sought in aims that are considered implied in the national law. It will then be difficult to remember to compare them to the aims of the underlying European legislation.

In **Italy**, literal transposition of directives occurs very often, which at first sight facilitates transposition and entails fewer risks, but in the longer run it complicates interpretation and application of the transposition legislation, for example by making the national legal system less coherent. The Council of State consistently opposed this mechanical transposition, of which its advice on the draft transposition act of the Telecommunications Directives provides an illustration.[48] In particular, the Council observed that the transposition method could be improved by translating the European texts into national texts, in such a way as to ensure the result and take into account the peculiarities of the internal administrative law.

In the **UK**, the 'copy-out' method of implementation is now widely used, which is said to allow courts and advocates to concentrate their attention on one instrument rather than two, and avoids disputes over whether a national measure properly implements the Community instrument. However, the British rapporteur observes that copy-out is less attractive when it is used to supplement pre-existing national provisions (e.g., on health and safety; unfair contract terms). The result is the appearance of over-regulation (usually blamed on Europe) and potential damage to legal certainty.[49] Furthermore, copy-out will not always be a practicable solution. In areas where Community instruments have only a limited impact on matters governed by national law (e.g., the licensing of credit institutions, or the content of national laws governing direct taxation or intellectual property rights), amendment of an existing national scheme may be the only realistic option. Where Community law largely governs the relevant subject-matter (e.g., the authorisation of medical products), it is considered preferable to bring the entire system of national legislation into line with European legislation. Where the impact is more marginal, the *ad hoc* adaptation with

---

[48] Advice No. 58/97 of 30 June 1997.
[49] See *R (Junttan Oy) v. Bristol Mag Ct* [2003] UKHL 55.

maintenance of the legislative system as long as possible may be preferable. The problems tend to come when an area of law is gradually taken over by Community principles and yet its original structure has not been revised. One example identified by the English courts has been the law relating to excise duty. Attempts to adapt 1970s legislation to more recent directives with a different conceptual starting-point have led to a complex and confusing statutory regime, which the courts have held, in some respects, not to properly implement those directives.[50] The rapporteur also observes that implementation of the Sixth VAT Directive is an unsuccessful example of *ad hoc* implementation (see further section 1.4.1), whereas implementation of habitat protection is a more successful example. Implementation of species protection is a good example of bringing the entire system of national legislation into line with European legislation (see section 1.4.2). Further, Section 2(2) of the European Communities Act 1972 authorises the government to use secondary legislation in order to amend primary legislation where it is necessary to do so in order to implement a Community obligation. There are exceptions, principally for measures increasing tax or imposing serious criminal penalties. Section 2(2) is used frequently, either on its own or as a shared legal basis for secondary legislation. The British rapporteur considers that by removing the need to find parliamentary time, it constitutes a useful and indeed essential way of ensuring the timely implementation of Community obligations in the UK. Constitutional challenges to the propriety of using Section 2(2) have occasionally been raised but have not generally been accepted by the courts.[51] Detailed guidelines for the use of Section 2(2) have been developed by the government; and all such measures are laid before parliament in order to give MPs the opportunity to object.

The **Swedish** rapporteur observes that adoption of the terminology of European legislation is always problematic since the European legislature seldom enters virgin territory and that the need for approximation of national legislation springs from this very fact. An additional problem occurred in particular at the beginning of Sweden's membership, concerning the fact that negotiations on European legislation are normally based on documents in a foreign language, as translations of the very latest version of a new directive – the one that is of interest to the negotiators – come very late. This may lead to a lack of interest in the native language version during negotiations, which is hard to remedy at a later stage.

In **Germany**, the federal government, the *Länder* or both may be responsible for transposition. Transposition requires the adoption of a law whenever an issue

---

[50] *R (Hoverspeed) v. CCE* [2002] EWHC 1630.
[51] See, e.g., *R v. S/S Industry ex parte Orange* [2001] 3 CMLR 781.

touches upon fundamental rights. Furthermore, the Constitutional Court held that parliament must assume responsibility for all important regulations, which it can do only by way of an Act of Parliament. Actually, transposition through the adoption of an administrative regulation is usually not easier than through an Act of Parliament, as according to Article 80 of the Constitution the competence to adopt such a regulation is to be based on a law setting out explicitly the contents, aims and limitations of the regulation. This also requires the approval of the *Bundesrat* (the Second Chamber of Parliament reuniting the governments of the *Länder*) and to obtain this, the federal government has to apply the same administrative procedure that is required for the adoption of an Act of Parliament. When a directive affects all *Länder* in the same way, the competent ministers usually sit down together and decide to elaborate a joint proposal for legislation. They do so on a voluntary basis and have even agreed to specialise in certain matters. Sometimes, it is actually the local communities, regions or other public authorities that have to transpose a directive, in which case numerous difficulties arise. In the case of shared competences of the federal government and the *Länder*, serious difficulties may have to be overcome in order to achieve satisfactory results.

Since the federal government is involved in the various stages of the European legislative process, it can determine whether transposition legislation is needed. Often, the existing national legislation already corresponds partly or entirely to the European rules. Literal transposition of an entire body of European legislation is hardly ever considered appropriate transposition, as this may require the use of different concepts as well as a different structure. Partial literal transposition may occur whenever this is compatible with the aim of the operation, for instance when a very detailed norm of European law is at issue. As much as possible, transposition must respect the existing legal language, which may only be left aside in the case that correct transposition within this linguistic framework is not possible. Within the same limits as apply to national legislation, it is possible that regulations and laws provide a dynamic reference to European legislation, but in practice this is very rare. In the case of belated transposition, the federal government communicates written advice to the responsible authorities on how to deal with cases affected by the directive, with a view to protecting the rights of individuals. Even if this is not compulsory and not corresponding to transposition requirements, this advice has shown its usefulness in 'softening' the consequences of belated transposition. Finally, other explanations have been given for the rather slow transposition of directives, in particular: the aim to do better or more than a directive actually requires[52] (in

---

[52] E.g., the aim of the federal government to establish a Federal Bureau for Nature Protection in the framework of the transposition of the Directive on the protection of singing birds.

view of the bad quality of European legislation or because existing legislation already covers a broader range of issues), maintaining the balance of the national legislative system, the quantity of legislation which goes beyond the administrative capacity to deal with its transposition and the time that may be required to find a solution that is coherent and compatible with an already elaborate legal system.

The **Spanish** rapporteur also points to the fact that it must first be established what authority is competent to transpose and apply a directive and that other decisions regarding the internal organisation of the state have to be taken. Furthermore, he doubts the legal admissibility of detailed directives that exclude true normative intervention by the Member States. In areas such as health and consumer protection, it regularly occurs that transposition is coupled with the adoption of rules the directive does not prescribe, with a view to improving the clarity of the system and the legislation. This is made clear in the preamble of the legislative act. Transposition may take place by way of the adoption of laws approved by parliament, or by legislative decrees and decree-laws approved by government. The latter does not occur very often. Most legislative decrees originate in the Framework Law 47/1985, which delegated to government the competence to transpose a number of specified directives with a view to accelerating the adaptation of the Spanish legal order to the *acquis communautaire*. Decree-laws may only be adopted in cases of extraordinary necessity and urgency, such as infringement proceedings against Spain for not having transposed a directive, transposition delays and obligations to act immediately in conformity with a Commission decision. The parliamentary procedure may be speeded up by applying a legislation urgency procedure, by legislative delegation to a parliamentary commission and by the approval of a bill in one reading.

In **Greece**, the system and terminology of European legislation are in principle respected in implementation. This has occurred in particular in respect of areas in which Greek legislation was fairly basic before its accession to the EC, such as environmental law, consumer protection, competition, transport, energy and health care. This has the advantage of speeding up the transposition process and of reducing the risk of a 'protectionist' interpretation by administrative authorities that sometimes discover, wrongly, margins of discretion in the use of different terminology. Yet, for reasons of clarity, legal certainty or uniformity one may sometimes prefer to stick to national legal terminology. This also occurs in respect of the transposition of very generally framed directive provisions or which explicitly leave discretion to the Member States. In the case that European legislation touches upon an area in which already a national system and terminology exist, it is either tried to transpose the directive into the national legal system or to reform the entire legislation. Evidently, these situations create most difficulties. Apart from that, it flows from Laws 945/1979 and 1338/1983, enacted with a view to enable accession to the EC, that the instrument *par excellence* for the transposition of directives is the regulatory decree, adopted by the President of the Republic at the proposal of the competent ministers. This possibility of legislative delegation is provided in Article 43, paragraph 2 of the Constitution. Yet, certain issues fall within the exclusive competence of the legislature, requiring the adoption of a formal law, and some, such as the creation of taxes, fall within the competence of the House of Representatives and cannot be delegated. Implementation by way of circulars does not occur. The scope of possible delegation may not always be clear, for instance as regards regulating the protection of public freedoms. The Constitution itself does not reserve particular issues to the regulatory power of the President or to other government authorities.

This has also led to a judgment by the Council of State in a case in which it was called upon to assess the refusal of the administration to establish a decree for the transposition of Directive 89/48/EEC concerning the mutual recognition of diplomas before the deadline of transposition had passed. Contrary to what was held by the claimants, the Council of State considered that, on the basis of the principle of institutional autonomy and thus of their own constitutional rules, the Member States may themselves choose the instruments to transpose a directive. So, the competence given to the President to transpose directives by way of a decree does not mean that the legislature may not adopt a law with a view to this, even after the deadline for implementation has passed. In the case of a regulatory decree, the Council of State indicates the provisions that have been laid down for the transposition of European rules and invites the government to show their European law origin in parentheses. This practice is not followed in the case of formal laws.

The **Belgian** Council of State is of the opinion that the use of terminology in national transposition legislation should stick as closely as possible to European terminology,[53] in particular as regards technical texts.[54] Such advice is prompted by concerns about comprehensibility and acting in conformity with higher rules. The Council is yet more watchful in the case of national legislation using a terminology which differs from the directive concerned and which already has specified meaning in national law.[55] In the case of vague European terminology, it is imperative that national transposition legislation is stated in unambiguous terms.[56] The coexistence of numerous language versions and the

---

[53] See, e.g., the Advice of 7 July 1994 and, more recently, that of 4 February 2004 in respect of Directive 2001/105/EC.
[54] Cf., Advice Nos. 35.982/1 to 35.985/1 of 30 October 2003.
[55] Cf., Advice No. 34.361/4.

fact that in Belgium laws have to be stated and adopted in the two national languages are considered complications in this regard. The Council of State generally also recommends that transposition come about by adapting existing legal provisions rather than by adopting autonomous texts leaving the existing provisions in force, possibly incompatible with European law, which may lead to legal insecurity.[57] Autonomous legislation may only be called for when the importance and scope of the subject at issue, touching upon various pieces of legislation, so requires.[58] Yet, ultimately this is a political choice to be made. This also goes for the partial transposition of directives, which is inevitable if a directive concerns issues that belong to the competence of the federal authorities, each having its own responsibility to incorporate it into their legal order. The partial nature of the transposition should, however, be clearly indicated. The advice of the Council of State on the proposed transposition of Directive 2003/87/EC of the European Parliament and of the Council of 13 October 2003 establishing a scheme for greenhouse gas emission allowance trading within the Community and amending Council Directive 96/61/EC,[59] illustrates that it does not encourage this kind of transposition, as it may affect the *effet utile* of the applicable legislation and the competences of the various federal authorities.

Sometimes, the Council of State may even propose that in the transposition of a particular directive account be taken of European acts for which the deadline of transposition has not yet passed.[60] Rather exceptionally, the Belgian authorities seize the opportunity of the transposition of a directive to replace the old law by a new one.[61] In some cases, they apparently assumed too easily that the adoption of transposition legislation was not necessary at all.[62] As regards accelerated transposition methods, the Council of State rejected the use of the referral method,[63] in particular when discretion is left to the Member States or when vague concepts need clarification. It only admitted this method with a view to establishing provisions exclusively addressed to the Member States. Public authorities are not in a position to use this method. As regards transposi-

---

[56] Cf., Advice No. 23.624. For concrete examples, see the Belgian report.

[57] See Advice of the Council of State on the proposed transposition law of Directive 97/81/EC concerning the framework agreement on part-time work.

[58] It was recommended, e.g., in respect of Directive 2001/42/EC.

[59] OJ 2003, L 275/32. Advice No. 36.057/4 of 24 November 2003.

[60] Advice No. 34.911/4 of 20 February 2003 is exemplary, concerning the transposition of Directive 1999/31/EC and the subsequent adoption of Decision 2003/33/EC.

[61] E.g., the transposition of Directives 90/531/EEC and 92/50/EEC (public markets).

[62] This occurred in the area of telecommunications, in respect of Directives 91/263/EEC and 93/97/EC.

[63] Advice No. 20.563/8 of 7 February 1991.

tion by delegation, the executive may already be empowered in a particular area, which then also includes the right to draw up transposition measures. Most often, however, specific empowerment is created geared towards the transposition of specific matters of European law, which may be done for reasons of technicality, the abundance of rules to be transposed, the blockage of the legislative process and the need for flexibility. Empowerment may be limited or unlimited in time and concern either specific or unspecific directives.[64] According to the rapporteur, in view of constitutional requirements and requirements of effectiveness, it would be advisable to have precise empowerment measures concerning the implementation of particular directives by administrative act and in the case of directives leaving a margin of discretion and requiring the intervention of the legislature; the empowering act should contain the relevant indications to this end. Legal concerns entailed by the delegation of transposition powers to the executive relate in particular to the fact that numerous empowering acts require confirmation by law within a specified time span.

The **French** rapporteur considers it best to convert Community legal concepts into national terms, with a view to taking account of national legal traditions and existing specific terminology. The French authorities also tend to leave the existing legislation as it is and to introduce only the modifications required in separate acts. This has been done, for instance, in respect of Directive 89/48/EEC, introducing a general system for the recognition of diplomas.[65] The legislature makes sure in particular that transposition does not affect the logic and coherence of the national law and that it respects common terminology, which is considered an essential element of legal certainty. Even though there is a preference for drafting the internal law completely in conformity with Community law, the problem remains that the administrative organisation must be able to do so. Practice shows that the problems this organisation is confronted with and the coordination between the various actors involved, are important reasons for the French delay in transposing directives. A more complete and systematic alignment of French rules with European rules would only aggravate this situation. The tendency to do more in implementation than a directive actually requires, is also a cause of delay.[66] This has occurred, for instance, in respect of Directives 1999/5/EC (telecommunications), 2000/52/EC (finan-

---

[64] See, for concrete examples, the Belgian report which is very detailed on the question of transposition by delegation.

[65] OJ 1989, L 19/16.

[66] See also the study of the Council of State of December 1989, attached as an annex to information report No. 182 of 11 January 2001 and the report on the state of transposition of Community directives, drawn up by Christian Philip, Member of Parliament, on behalf of the EU Delegation of the National Assembly, No. 1009 (2002-2003).

cial relations) and 90/167/EC (medical products for animals).[67] Article 38 of the Constitution provides for the possibility of applying an accelerated transposition method in areas that are normally covered by laws in the form of government decrees adopted on the authorisation of parliament during a limited period of time. Until recently, the use thereof was exceptional, but Law 2001-1 of 3 January 2001 empowered the government to transpose 46 directives in this way. A short while ago, the Council of State was asked for advice on a law that is to empower the government to transpose another 20 directives in this way. Because of its expeditiousness and simplicity, this procedure has clearly been resorted to with a view to reducing the delay in transposition. Even though it seems to be applied foremost in the case of technical directives that are not politically sensitive (but see also the next section), the use of this procedure has been heavily criticised because it excludes parliament from the transposition process.

1.4   Case study: transposing and applying the Bird and Habitat Directives and the Sixth VAT Directive

What problems have arisen in the framework of the transposition and application of the Sixth VAT Directive and the Bird and Habitat Directives? What were/ are the causes for this and, if solved, how has this been done? By what factors can the various national experiences with these directives be explained and what conclusions can be drawn from the comparison of the situation in the different Member States? (questions 1.2.5-1.2.7 of the questionnaire)

1.4.1 *The Sixth VAT Directive*[68]

Turning now to a first example of how the transposition of a concrete piece of European legislation has been dealt with, it appears that the transposition and application of the Sixth VAT Directive has encountered problems in particular in those Member States that chose to retain, to some extent, the system, structure and terminology of the national law on this type of taxation (**Finland, Austria, the Netherlands, Italy, the UK**). This can be taken as an indication that there is at least some kind of correlation between the method of transposition or implementation technique chosen and the subsequent interpretation and

---

[67] OJ 1999, L 91/10; OJ 2000, L 193/75; and OJ 1990, L 92/42, respectively.

[68] Sixth Council Directive 77/388/EEC of 17 May 1977 on the harmonisation of the laws of the Member States relating to turnover taxes – Common system of value added tax: Uniform basis of assessment, OJ 1977, L 145/1.

application problems of European and transposition legislation that national courts are confronted with.

The problems that occurred in **Finland** concern the fact that the VAT Act was drafted some years before Finland acceded to the EU. Even though this Act was based on the directive, in many cases the legislature did not want to follow the European system, partly because of different policy choices, partly because Finland was not expected to participate fully in the internal market. After Finland's accession, the conflicts between the national Act and the directive had to be resolved.[69] Since the Finnish Act differs from the directive as to its structure as well as in many of its expressions, there is constant tension between them and the directive is often relied upon as a basis for deliberation and is frequently referred to in the decisions of the Supreme Administrative Court.[70] On the whole, however, there is considered to be no conflict between the VAT Act and the directive, and the directive has been directly applied only exceptionally. The impact of European law and the ambiguous nature of the national Act have increased the number of VAT cases, the fiscal treatment of financing and real-estate transactions turning out to be the most ambiguous areas. For those decisions, application of European law has become the rule rather than the exception. So far, the Supreme Administrative Court has referred only one VAT case to the ECJ.[71]

The **Austrian** report first of all points to the fact that in adopting the new VAT Act 1994,[72] which implements the Sixth VAT Directive, the structure and the terminology of the VAT Act of 1972 were upheld, not those of the directive. An example of the problems this may give rise to relates to the fact that Articles 5 and 6 of the Directive define as taxable transactions the supply of goods and the supply of services. The VAT Act 1994 provides that the supply of goods, the supply of services and self-consumption are chargeable events. Self-consumption is defined as the use of goods that are or, until then, were used for the assets of the business for private means or the supply of goods or services by the taxable person in the context of his business for private use. In its judgment in the *Seeling* case,[73] the ECJ clarified that the private use – self-consumption – of a building is not covered by Article 13B(b) of the directive, which

---

[69] Cf., also the judgment in the infringement Case C-169/00 *Commission v. Finland*, ECR [2002] I-2433.

[70] European law played an important part in one out of four of the approximately 80 VAT decisions published by the Court between 1 January 1997 and 30 June 1999. After that period, the importance of European law has increased rather than decreased.

[71] Case C-101/00 *Tulliasiamies and Antti Siilin*, ECR [2002] I-7487, primarily concerning car tax, but containing also a question about the VAT payable on car tax.

[72] Federal Gazette No. 663/1994.

[73] Case C-269/00 *Seeling*, ECR [2003] I-4101.

grants tax exemption for the leasing or letting of immovable property. A draft amendment of the VAT Act 1994 is now supposed to eliminate the exemption for self-consumption, adopts the system of the directive on this point and follows the wording of the directive. Secondly, it is noted that problems may arise from the fact that the same wording is used in an EC directive and in national legislation though having a different meaning from that in national legislation. This became clear for instance, as regards the meaning of the term 'leasing or letting', which the ECJ clarified in the *Goed Wonen* and *Sinclair Collis* cases.[74] In its decision of 30 October 2003, the Supreme Administrative Court pointed out that for the purpose of VAT the administration was wrong in assuming that 'leasing or letting' was to be understood according to the applicable national law.[75] Thirdly, questions may arise when national legislation refers to other national legislation.[76] As far as no solution has been provided for by the legislature, the Federal Ministry of Finance issues instructions on all relevant questions arising in the application of tax law. In this context, the most important questions relating to European law are dealt with, too.

In **the Netherlands**, the Sixth VAT Directive was implemented while maintaining as far as possible the system of the law as set up in 1968. This – wrong – point of departure for implementing the directive caused interpretation and application problems, for instance regarding the concept of 'taxpayer', which is defined differently in Dutch law.[77] As a result, the concept of 'entrepreneur' in turnover tax law gained a very different meaning in the case law than in other areas of Dutch law. Since this concerns a politically sensitive area and the basic principles of Dutch VAT legislation are at issue, amendments are difficult to realise and thus no national legislative measures have been announced.

In **Italy**, the transposition of the Sixth VAT Directive[78] has raised definition problems as to the principle of territoriality applicable to the payment of VAT on the provision of services. There are numerous exceptions to the rule that VAT is paid in the state in which the service is performed, provided for in the directive. Yet, it may be difficult to establish the contents of the services at issue. For example, the definition of 'professional services' in the national law

---

[74] Case C-326/99 *Goed Wonen*, ECR [2001] I-6831 and Case C-275/01 *Sinclair Collis*, ECR [2003] I-5965, respectively.

[75] 2000/15/0109.

[76] See, e.g., the decision of the Austrian Supreme Administrative Court of 19 December 2002, 2001/15/0093, concerning Section 12 of the VAT Act 1994 in relation to Art. 17 (para. 6) of Directive 77/388/EEC.

[77] According to the Directive, 'taxable person' is to mean any person who independently carries out in any place any economic activity; in Dutch law, *de ondernemer* [the entrepreneur].

[78] Through the legislative decree provided for by Ministerial Decree No. 633 of 26 October 1972.

seems to differ from that in the directive. The ECJ has made it clear that the list of professional services contained in Article 9(2) of the directive is exhaustive and excludes arbitrators,[79] whereas on the basis of the wording of the national law these are included. Another interpretation issue relates to the translation of 'fixed establishment' by 'stable organisation' in the national law, terms which are not each other's equivalents. At the judicial level, interpreting the national law in the light of its aim, which is transposition of the directive, solves these problems.

The **British** rapporteur states that the implementation of Directive 77/388 was considered by parliament in 1977, when the government majority was slender and defeat on the Finance Bill would have precipitated a general election. Whether for this reason or because of departmental inertia, Ministers sought to make the minimum possible changes to the pre-existing system. According to the rapporteur, the result has been confusing, and productive of much litigation. He indicates two main reasons for the difficulties in interpretation. The first stems from the fact that a number of legal concepts have different meanings in Member States with civil law jurisdiction, on the one hand, and Member States with common law jurisdictions, on the other. Concepts like 'consideration', 'agency', and 'tax avoidance' are mentioned as examples of this. It is considered likely that the drafters of European legislation are lawyers from civil law jurisdictions and the concepts they use cannot always be directly translated into equivalent common law concepts. The second difficulty is said to stem from the differing approaches to the drafting of tax legislation. In the UK, tax legislation has always been strictly construed and is, therefore, drafted in precise form. The European directives, on the contrary, are of a more general nature and have to be construed purposively; this is less instinctive for UK tax lawyers and the UK judiciary who are, nonetheless, conscious of the need for uniform interpretation across the Community. These difficulties cannot be blamed on incorrect or incomplete national implementating legislation because it has become increasingly common for taxable persons here to rely directly on the directives rather than on the national implementing legislation. The British rapporteur further observes that interpretational problems of the two types identified above in section 1.1 have arisen over the Sixth VAT Directive. He states in particular that interpretational problems arise because the VAT Directive has been created by VAT specialists who live on a VAT island. This is illustrated by the fact that 'economic activities' (roughly equivalent to 'business') has one meaning in the VAT Directive and another in the Competition Law Directive. Another example is that 'insurance agent' and 'insurance broker' are undefined

---

[79] Case C-145/96 *Von Hoffman v. Finanzamt Trier,* ECR [1997] I-4857.

in the VAT Directive and that it came as a surprise to those responsible for tax compliance in the insurance industry that the Insurance Intermediairies Directive (Directive 77/92) contains definitions of the terms.[80] This directive must have been in the process of being drafted when the VAT Directive was going through the system. Surely there could have been some cross referencing to guide the users of the VAT Directive? Furthermore, interpretational problems have arisen, because some problems of European law get lost in translation. Taking Article 5.4(c) of the VAT Directive as an example, the term 'contract of commission' (which is understood to be a civil-law term) has been translated into English as 'a contract under which commission is payable'. Another example concerns Article 13A.1(1), which exempts 'organisations with aims of a trade union nature': was that phrase a faithful translation of the phrase 'organisations du nature syndicale'? The matter had to be referred to the ECJ.[81] The expression (loosely translated from the French) 'organisations recognised as having a social character' in Article 13A.1(g) of the directive was translated by the official translator into the English language as 'organisations recognised as charitable'.

In **France**, the Bill aimed at transposing the Sixth VAT Directive was rejected because of the loss of sovereignty it was considered to entail for the French legislature, resulting from the fact that the directive was too detailed and in fact resembled a regulation. Later, notably Law 92-667 of 17 July 1992 transposed the directive. The application of this text gives rise to a paradox, namely, that the French interpretation of this directive meets with the case law of the ECJ evolving in a direction which goes counter to the French legal tradition which inspired the text of the directive.

In **Portugal**, the transposition of the Sixth VAT Directive did not entail specific problems since it was possible to introduce the European law aspects in the general rules of this taxation, which was being newly established. Yet, preliminary questions have been posed concerning its interpretation. In **Greece**, no specific problems seem to have occurred either, the directive having been transposed by formal Law 1642/1986, as Article 78 of the Constitution requires for the creation of taxes. Since the *Comunidades Autónomas* in **Spain** have no legislative power as regards this kind of taxation, transposition of the Sixth VAT Directive took place by means of a statc law.[82] An interpretation problem occurred pursuant to an error in the official translation into Spanish; what was thus considered by some to be a general exoneration clause in the directive was transformed into a

---

[80] See Case *Century Life v. Customs and Excise Commissioners,* [2001] STC 34 (CA).
[81] Case *Institute of the Motor Industry v. Customs and Excise Commissioners,* [1998] STC 1219.
[82] Law 37/1992 of 28 December, BOE, No. 312.

specific exception clause in the national legislation. The judgment of the ECJ in the *Amengual v. Far* case[83] is said to have made clear that the directive left it to the Member States to choose for one or the other possibility.

The **Belgian** rapporteur observes also that the implementation of the Sixth VAT Directive has raised no particular interpretation problems for the legislative and administrative sections of the Belgian Council of State, other than those which are encountered more generally in the application of the positive law in general and of European law in particular. Yet, it should be noted that, because of reasons of urgency, the draft bill which led to the Law of 27 December 1977, aiming at the transposition of this directive and which amended the Belgian VAT Code to this end, was not submitted to the legislative section of the Council of State. The administrative section has no competence on this matter. The advice was given on texts amending the VAT Code posterior to 1977 does not mention any particular difficulties with the interpretation of the Sixth VAT Directive either. The legislative section has merely dealt with, often minor, problems relating to the enforcement of the directive and has also, in some cases, discussed the scope of particular provisions.[84]

In conclusion, it may be observed that problems of alignment of the European and national legal systems come clearly to the fore in the transposition and application of European legislation when the national legislature sticks too much or too long to the national system, structure and (interpretation of) terminology. This approach may, however, impose itself more in certain politically sensitive areas, such as tax policy, than in others.

1.4.2 *The Bird and Habitat Directives*[85]

Looking at a second concrete example, it appears that in quite a number of Member States, the transposition of the Bird and Habitat Directives has been seriously delayed or encountered problems. Internal reasons account for this as well as reasons of a substantive nature. It is particularly clear that the federal state structures of **Germany**, **Austria**, **Belgium** and **Italy** have complicated their transposition.

Focusing first on the latter aspect, the failure of the **German** federal government to adopt a framework law thus made it impossible for the *Länder* to do their part of the job. More generally, transposition deadlines can often not be

---

[83] Case C-12/98 *Amengual v. Far,* ECR [2000] I-527.
[84] See the Belgian report for details.
[85] Directive 79/409/EEC of 2 April 1979 on the conservation of wild birds, OJ 1979, L 103/1, and Directive 92/43/EEC of 21 May 1992 on the conservation of natural habitats and of wild fauna and flora, OJ 1992, L 206/7, respectively.

met because of Germany's federal structure. In the **Austrian** legal system, the competence for implementation of the two directives generally lies with the *Länder*, but the directives also pertain to questions that are regulated in the Forestry Act, which falls within the competence of the Federation, and to the hunting and fishing regulations, which again fall within the competence of the *Länder*.[86] In **Belgium**, the protection and conservation of nature, hunting, river fishing and fish farming have been transferred to the competence of the regions, whereas the federal government has remained competent for these matters as far as they relate to the territorial sea. This division of competences has raised difficulties. A large number of laws, decrees, and regulations, both at the level of the regions and of the federal government, had to be modified and adopted in order to fulfil the requirements of the Bird and Habitat directives.[87] This has resulted in a rather fragmented legal framework, in respect of which the legislative department of the Council of State has held that, at least in certain respects, transparency should be improved. Moreover, the Council of State has criticised the fact that quite some wide implementing powers have been delegated to the executive.[88] More recently, there has been a tendency to leave the basic regulation to the legislature, which is illustrated by the Decree of the Walloon Region of 6 December 2001 relating to the conservation of Natura 2000 sites. In **Italy** too, the transposition of these directives raised problems primarily as to the delimitation of the competences of the state and the regions and the form of the transposition itself, which led to a number of decisions by the Constitutional Court.[89] Yet, in the decentralised system of **Spain** it seems that such problems did not occur, the directives having been transposed in particular by way of framework legislation adopted by the state.[90]

---

[86] For a very brief survey on the implementation, cf., Weber, *Stand und Entwicklung des österreichischen Naturschutzrechts*, Juristische Blätter 2000, 701 (703). A comprehensive description can be found in Ennöckl, *Natura 2000. Die Vogelschutz- und Fauna-Flora-Habitat-Richtlinie und ihre Umsetzung im österreichischen Naturschutzrecht*, Vienna, Verlag Österreich, 2002. For a survey on the legal aspects of transposition of those two directives, see Mauerhofer, 'Zur Umsetzung der Vogelschutzrichtlinie in Österreich. Rechtliche Aspekte', in: Karner/Mauerhofer/Ranner, *Handlungsbedarf für Österreich zur Umsetzung der EU-Vogelschutzrichtlinie*, Umweltbundesamt (ed.), Report No. 144, 1997, 2nd edn., 112.

[87] See the Belgian report for details.

[88] Advice No. 33.061/3 of 23 April 2002.

[89] As regards the Habitat Directive (transposed by Art. 4 of Law No. 146 of 1994 and Ministerial Decree No. 357 of 8 September 1997), decision No. 425 of 1999. As regards the Bird Directive (transposed by Law No. 157 of 11 February 1992), decisions No. 226 and No. 227 of 4 July 2003.

[90] Royal Decree 1497/86 of 6 June, BOE, No. 173, p. 26224 and Royal Decree 4/89 of 27 March, BOE, No. 74, p. 8262, both transposing the Bird Directive. Royal Decree 1997/95 of 7 December, BOE, No. 310, p. 37310, transposing the Habitat Directive.

In **Finland**, another state-specific matter complicated the transposition of these directives. That is, a major problem was that not only did Finnish legislation have to be adapted to the European directives, but the European system had to be adapted to the circumstances of Finnish nature as well. The annexes of the directives thus had to be supplemented with references to boreal and arctic species and nature types. The directives were implemented by means of amendments to the Nature Conservation Act and other acts, which entered into force in 1997, after the deadline for implementation had expired. Finnish legislation had to be amended in order to extend the legal effects of protection to areas surrounding Natura 2000 sites, whereas according to the national legislation conservation had legal effects only as regards the area that had been designated as protected. This also entailed expanded use of environmental impact analyses. The most important consequence of the directives is the establishment of Natura 2000 areas. On 20 August 1998, the government decided to propose and designate 439 sites under the Bird Directive and 1325 sites under the Habitat Directive to be included in the Natura 2000 network, the area of which corresponds to the combined area of Belgium and the Netherlands. In May 2002, the government proposed 289 new areas or redefinitions of old areas to the network. The Supreme Administrative Court received 1,241 appeals involving some 750 sites, most of which consisted of demands for sites to be withdrawn or reduced, but there were also many appeals requesting sites to be expanded or added. The total number of appellants exceeded 5,000, including owners of the land and water areas concerned, local authorities and organisations representing the interests of nature conservation. The provisions on species and natural habitats of the directives were of key importance as the selection criteria were not transposed into national law and the Court had to apply directly the relevant provisions of the directives. The total number of decisions issued (mainly on 14 June 2000) was 694. Their aggregated text comprises over 40,000 pages. In about 7 per cent of all decisions, the government decision was annulled either in whole or in part. The government decision of 2003 to supplement the Natura 2000 network led to 68 new appeals to the Supreme Administrative Court. These cases are still pending. Finally, a special implementation problem concerned Article 12(1)(d) of Directive 92/43/EEC and the protection of the flying squirrel (a Siberian species living in no other EU country but Finland).

In **Greece**, the directives were transposed by way of ministerial decrees, adopted on the basis of the authorisation under Article 2 of Law 1338/1983, but the constitutionality of this delegation of authorisation may be questioned. In **France**, also, the Bird and Habitat Directives were transposed in particular by way of Decree 2001-321 of 11 April 2001, adopted on the basis of the empowering Law of 3 January 2001, discussed above in section 1.4. Law 2003-

591 of 2 July 2003 explicitly confirmed the decree. The establishment of Natura 2000 areas has raised most problems and led to three infringement proceedings of the Commission against France. The reasons for the delay in implementation can be traced back to the wide protests that the Natura 2000 project raised and the fact that the Commission required the classification of such areas without being able to specify the future legal consequences of such a classification. The transposition by way of decree has been fiercely criticised given the fact that parliament was not involved in issues that affect many people because of the many sectors of activity concerned.

In addition to what was already observed above in respect of **Belgium**, the implementation and application of the Bird and Habitat Directives have caused numerous problems in this Member State and they are at the origin of abundant case law, both of the legislative and the administrative departments of the Council of State.[91] Many difficulties, however, concern the belated or insufficient transposition of these directives, leading to case law on the direct applicability of directive provisions that were not properly transposed into Belgian law, or to pure and simple application problems not having anything to do with particular interpretation problems in the sense of this report. These application problems can be explained by a number of factors, some of which are said to be particular to Belgium, such as its four levels of power (see above), the relative smallness of its territory, the great urbanism, and the holding on to deep-rooted local traditions (such as the shooting of birds) which are in conflict with directive requirements. Other factors are more common to the Member States and are encountered in particular in regions in economic difficulty, such as the obstacles that the implementation of the directives may pose for certain developments or the necessity to mobilise a high administrative capacity in order to respect the directives' requirements. Some interpretation conflicts that have arisen between the Commission and the Belgian government have been dealt with by the ECJ in the framework of infringement proceedings against Belgium because of belated transposition of the directives.[92] More generally, the difficulties have been resolved in quite a variety of ways, such as by formal and informal contacts between the Belgian administrations and the Commission services involved, by these administrations taking account of the Guide of the European Commission 'Conservation of areas Natura 2000 – The dispositions of Article 6 of the Directive 92/43/EEC on the conservation of natural habitats and of wild fauna and flora', by better consultation between the Belgian administra-

---

[91] See the Belgian report for a fairly elaborate account of this case law.

[92] *Inter alia*, Case C-324/01 *Commission v. Belgium*, ECR [2002] I-11197; Case C-415/01 *Commission v. Belgium*, judgment of 27 February 2003, not yet reported. See the Belgian report for a detailed discussion of this case law.

tions, by taking account of the ECJ's case law, etc. In particular the pro-active organisation of informal meetings on specific aspects of the directives between the Belgian administrations and the Commission's services seems to have led to satisfactory contacts and results, by putting the emphasis on collaboration rather than on a coercive and purely regulatory approach. The Council of State itself has also contributed, at least partly, to solving the difficulties, by giving, in its advice, a complete and profound account of the obligations that these directives impose on the Member States.[93]

According to the **Austrian** report, the problem as regards the implementation of the Habitat Directive arises mainly from the complicated system of nominating potential areas for the protection by the Member States and the establishment of the definitive list of protected areas by the Commission. Member States have to comply with many obligations in the period before a site is finally listed as a site of European importance.[94] These obligations also apply when the Member State failed to name a site but should have done so, or classified an area that is not large enough. It is hard to establish these obligations in a general way in the Nature Protection Act of the *Länder*, which entails the necessity of direct application of European law.[95] The *Land* of Lower Austria nominated one third of its territory. In its judgment of 27 June 2002, the Administrative Court had to apply the 'old' Styrian Nature Protection Act in order to comply with the obligations arising from the two directives. The government authority and the Court had to examine whether the designation of areas by the government of the *Land* complied with the directive requirements. In this decision, the Administrative Court accepted the necessity of direct application of the directives,[96] thus following the case law of the ECJ. Yet, it held that the specific question whether the Habitat Directive is directly applicable in 'poten-

---

[93] See, e.g., Advice No. 30.537/4 and following.

[94] Cf., Case C-57/89 *Commission v. Germany (Leybucht)*, ECR [1991] I-883; Case C-355/90 *Commission v. Spain (Santona)*, ECR [1993] I-4221 and Case C-166/97 *Commission v. French Republic*, ECR [1999] I-1719.

[95] On the discussion concerning the possibility of direct application in cases where this leads to disadvantages for citizens, see Ennöckl, *Natura 2000*, 59; Madner, 'Naturschutz und Europarecht', in: Potacs (ed.), *Beiträge zum Kärntner Naturschutzrecht*, 17 [56]; Mauerhofer, *Das Schutzgebietssystem 'Natura 2000' nach den Richtlinien 79/409/EWG ('Vogelschutz-Richtlinie') und 92/43/EWG ('Fauna-Flora-Habitat-Richtlinie')*, RdU (environmental law) 1999, 83. In the implementation of the directives at stake the ECJ seems to follow the approach of an 'objective effect' of directives, thus deviating from the line that directives cannot produce effects detrimental to the citizen.

[96] In a decision of 23 October 1995, 95/10/0108, the Administrative Court denied the direct applicability of the Habitat Directive (because the time limit for the classification of areas had not expired) and did not examine the case in the light of the Bird Directive, which was criticised in Austrian literature; cf., Ennöckl, *Natura 2000*, 58; in its decision of 27 June 2002, 99/10/0159,

tial habitat areas' was not yet sufficiently clarified in the case law.[97] It concluded that the government authority was obliged to examine whether the area at stake fulfilled the criteria for special protection areas. As the administrative Act lacked sufficient reasoning on this, the Court annulled the act.

The **Spanish** and **Portuguese** rapporteurs point to other substantive problems of the directives. In particular, the vagueness of certain terms and concepts in these directives have led to divergent interpretations of the Commission and various Member States, which also led to infringement proceedings.[98] In **Portugal**, the transposition of the Bird and Habitat Directives came about by establishing new legislation[99] since there was no national legislation yet on this matter. Consequently, the framework of the national legislation practically coincides with that of the directives. The application of the Habitat Directive caused practical difficulties because of its use of excessively vague concepts. The more concrete concepts of the Bird Directive were more easily integrated in national law and applied, despite the fact that a more complete and systematic protection regulation was adopted only in 1999.

In **the Netherlands**, until recently virtually no implementation measures were taken with a view to protecting the areas concerned, which leads not only to substantive questions of interpretation, but also to questions of consistent interpretation and direct effect. A bill – prompted also by infringement proceedings of the Commission against the Dutch State – aims at transposing the provisions at issue quite literally and is now being discussed in parliament. Since this way of transposition will lead to an accumulation of rules, the bill has been criticised and its discussion stagnates.

In the **UK**, the Bird Directive was implemented by a modern and comprehensive piece of legislation, drafted with the specific aim of giving effect to the directive and to the Council of Europe Convention on which it was based. According to the British rapporteur, implementation of this directive and of the species protection provisions of Directive 92/43 has not given rise to significant difficulties. Where habitat protection is concerned, there is a contrast between

---

the Court stressed that the question at stake in the former decision was the prolongation of the validity of a licence granted before Austria's accession to the EU, and therefore was not the same as in the latter case.

[97] Cf., Gellermann, *Natura 2000. Europäisches Habitatschutzrecht und seine Durchführung in der Bundesrepublik Deutschland*, 121.

[98] Case C-355/90 *Commission v. Spain,* ECR [1993] I-4221, in which Spain was held to have infringed the Bird Directive.

[99] Decree Law No. 75/91 of 14 February 1991 transposes the Bird Directive and Decree Law 280/94 of 5 November 1994 transposes the Habitat Directive. Decree Law 140/99 of 24 April 1999 contains a revision of this transposition legislation, reuniting the transposition of both Directives.

the traditional British approach of balancing conflicting interests and the Community approach which requires conservation to have the highest priority. That contrast was brought home to the government and to environmental lawyers by case C-44/95 *R v. S/S Environment ex parte RSPB (Lappel Bank)*.[100] Directive 92/43 has been implemented by Regulations which preserve the pre-existing legal framework (based on the exercise of administrative discretion), but requires those discretions to be exercised in accordance with the specific requirements of Community law.

In conclusion, this short survey of the implementation of the Bird and Habitat Directives shows that problems of alignment of the European and national legal systems may originate both in state-specific factors, such as the state structure, nature, regional economic circumstances, etc., and in European factors such as the defective quality of the European legislation to be transposed. This can only be remedied by taking the appropriate action both at the national and European levels.

2. DEALING WITH INTERPRETATION PROBLEMS

We will now turn to the ways and means in which the interpretation problems sketched in the previous section may be prevented and dealt with. The fact that the broader angle of interpretation problems has been taken and not that of mere quality problems explains why we will not limit ourselves here to considering how Member States can contribute to a better quality of European legislation (and thereby to the prevention of interpretation and implementation problems) by way of *ex ante* examination of European legislation, but why we also seek to establish the attitude of the national courts towards European law and to find out how they deal with the uncertainties in that law. To this end, not only the relevance of *travaux préparatoires* and other interpretation aids will be discussed, but also the recourse to different language versions, the considerations behind the use of the preliminary rulings procedure and its aims and the existing forms of cooperation in this regard.

A preliminary observation, made by the **Italian** rapporteur, is that even though uniform interpretation and implementation of European law plays a central role in the national legal orders and is a fundamental value that Member States try to achieve, interpretation is not a purely mechanic but partly a creative process. Hence, a differentiated interpretation and thus transposition of one and the same rule should, in his view, be accepted to a certain extent, as a

---

[100] Case C-44/95 *R v. S/S Environment ex parte RSPB (Lappel Bank)*, ECR [1996] I-3805.

physiological characteristic of even a system such as the European one, in which the national courts must try to bring the different national rules back to a uniform interpretation of the European legal rule from which they ensue.

2.1   *Ex ante* examination of European legislation

What possibilities are there in the Member States of ex ante examination of European legislation? How can they contribute to the prevention of interpretation and implementation problems? (questions 1.3.1-1.3.3. Suggestions regarding advice on European legislation are discussed in Chapter 3, section 2.)

Not all national reports contain information on the existing possibilities for *ex ante* examination of European legislation. Yet, it appears that in some states there are highly developed structures for this (**Finland**), whereas in other states such structures are far more limited (**Greece**) or at least less used (**Italy**).

In **Finland**, an intensive dialogue between parliament and government takes place as early as possible in the European legislative process, and is continued until the matter is finally decided by the Council. Within parliament, specialised committees and the Grand Committee acting as the European affairs committee are involved in this dialogue. This process provides transparency in the national position on the development of European legislation and gives parties interested such as management and labour and NGOs the possibility to participate in it. The system also forces the government to analyse transposition problems already at the beginning of negotiations at the European level and thus contributes to avoiding or mitigating legislative quality problems at the national level. According to the principle of parliamentary accountability, it is understood that the government follows the opinion of the Grand Committee so far as questions within the constitutional competence of parliament are concerned. Furthermore, negotiation positions of the ministries at the EU Council and its preparatory organs are coordinated by a special structure under the Office of the Prime Minister. In this coordination process, legal questions relating to Commission proposals are discussed and analysed in a special legal working group, for which the Unit of European Law of the Ministry of Justice provides secretariate assistance. Ministries can also independently seek the legal opinion of the Ministry of Justice on Commission proposals. In the working group and in the written opinions of the European Law Unit, the Commission proposals are analysed not only from a national point of view but also in the European law context.

In **Austria** as well, the competent ministries have to inform parliament – *de lege lata* – on EU legislative initiatives. Moreover, the Constitutional Service of the Federal Chancellery is usually involved in the legislative process and is to consider the legislative quality of proposed European rules. Upon accession, the 'Legislative Guidelines' were also amended with a view to the transposition of European law.[101] Yet, a centralised national institution can only sufficiently deal with the huge amount of legislative proposals if it has adequate staff.

If the **Swedish** Law Council observes errors in the implementation of a directive when scrutinising a transposition bill, the government's bill is almost always rectified in order to comply with the directive.

The **Italian** Council of State may examine, upon the request of the President of the Council of Ministers, EU legislative proposals,[102] but this does not occur often. Article 1 bis of Law No. 86 of 9 March 1989 provides that the EU proposals are sent to parliament and to the regions, and that they can address their observations to government. This provision has not had much effect either.

In **Greece**, no mechanism of facultative or compulsory *ex ante* examination of European legislation has been established. The Council of State is not consulted during the legislative process, as the Constitution limits its consultative function to an ex ante check of the legality of regulatory decrees. The recent amendment of the Constitution did not lead to acceptance of the proposal to have the Council's consultative function extended to proposals of European legislation, but explicitly provided for informing parliament on such proposals. In practice there are also some interministerial committees that examine proposals for European legislation, but they do not deal in detail with the legal aspects thereof. In checking the legality of regulatory decrees – which are most often used for the transposition of European legislation –, the Council of State considers the interpretation questions that the European text will entail as well as the quality of the national transposition legislation. This check elucidates the various problems that have to be solved, such as terminology problems, compatibility with national law, etc., and may influence the drafting of the decree. Yet, it is also noted that interpretation difficulties often occur only in a concrete situation and that the facts of the case enable the discovery of the different aspects of a legal rule.

In **Belgium**, the general view is that the tie-up between Community law and Belgian law would be better ensured if both the legislative and the administrative authorities responsible for the transposition of directives were more involved in their elaboration and drafting. One of the difficulties the Belgian negotiators have to take into account during the process of preparing directives

---

[101] EU-Addendum zu den legistischen Richtlinien 1990, to be found at <www.bka.gv.at> ('Legistik'). Cf., also Obenaus, *Gemeinschaftsrechtlichen Anforderungen an die österreichische Legistik*, JRP 1999, p. 111, and Bußjäger and Kleiser (eds.), *Legistik und Gemeinschaftsrecht*, 2001.

[102] Provided by Law No. 127 of 15 March 1997, Art. 17, para. 28.

are the peculiarities of the Belgian federal system. To facilitate this, a cooperation agreement was concluded on 8 March 1994 between the state, the communities, and the regions. Different initiatives have also been taken in order to
increase the role of the parliamentary assemblies in the elaboration of Community legislation. Yet, even though there is now more awareness of the effects of
European legislation on the internal law, their involvement in the creation of
European legislation is still rather disappointing, both because of the insufficient effectiveness of the procedures provided for and their non-obligatory nature. These procedures include, *inter alia*, the submission by the government of
an annual report on the implementation and application of the European Treaties and the creation of a federal advice committee charged with European affairs, composed of 10 MPs, 10 senators, and 10 MEPs. Up to now, this
committee has failed to proceed in a systematic way on the scrutiny of directive
proposals and their implementation. The permanent commissions within the
parliaments have also failed to do so. In the cases in which the federal advice
committee has selected documents for further examination by the permanent
commissions, these have failed to give the appropriate follow-up. In 2000, this
procedure was relaunched by appointing an *europromoteur* within each permanent commission who is also a member of the federal advice committee. In
conclusion, it can be observed that the prior intervention of the Belgian parliaments is more directed towards the political implications of the proposed Community measures and directives than towards their legal or technical feasibility.

More in general, the Belgian rapporteur points to the extreme complexity of
the internal (executive) procedures that have been devised to establish the Belgian position within the Commission and the Council of Ministers, the difficulties of positioning the legislative assemblies in this context, and the insufficient
attention that is given within the executive organs to the coordination of the
stages of preparation and of transposition of European directives. The legislative department of the Council of State does not play any role in the adoption
process of European legislation. Only at the transposition stage is the Council
under an obligation to give its advice. Different proposals to involve the Council of State at an earlier stage have remained without effect. According to the
rapporteur, such involvement would also entail a number of difficulties, most
fundamentally as regards the effectiveness of such intervention and the risk of
reinforcing the weight of national traditions in the decision-making process.
Moreover, if the intervention is directed in particular towards ensuring the coherence of European law or its compatibility with the Treaties or general principles of law, the Council of State does not seem to be the most appropriate
institution for doing this. Other difficulties concern the timing of such consultation and its object and modalities. The Belgian federal government is not in
favour of such an extension of the powers of the Council of State, in particular

because such consultation would prolong the adoption process of directives. Furthermore, a problem of authority of advice might present itself if each Member State were to provide for a similar national consultation.

The **German** rapporteur is of the opinion that if the national legislature were to have sufficient time during the negotiation process to consider details, the legal check exercised by the legal services of the Union and by national experts would be sufficient to maintain an adequate level of quality of European legislation. The influence of the Federal Administrative Court on European legislation is rather marginal, given that none of its five branches plays an active role in the legislative process and that it has no consultative section comparable to that of the Councils of State in other countries. Nonetheless, the supreme courts do have some indirect influence on the legislative process, as they may call upon the government and the legislature to take action when they consider that existing legislation or the lack thereof may lead to unreasonable or unacceptable results. Such an influence may even flow stronger from the case law of the Constitutional Court, which often appeals directly to the legislature to find a solution to a specific problem, sketching the contours of the solution in order to be in conformity with the Constitution, while respecting the discretion left to the legislature. The Federal Minister of Justice may also ask advice on a particular piece of proposed legislation and the Federal Administrative Court may submit remarks or observations to the Minister on certain law proposals, of which it has gained knowledge in an informal way.

Law does not prescribe consultation of the **Spanish** Council of State on Commission proposals. The rapporteur considers that imposing such an obligation would not only slow down the definition of the national position, but also entail an increased workload for the Council of State.

According to Article 88-4 of the **French** Constitution, introduced pursuant to constitutional Law 99-49 of 25 January 1999, the government has to submit all Community legislative proposals to parliament. Other kinds of documents may also be submitted to them. This brings with it that the Council of State has to examine first whether a proposed Community act is of a legislative nature or not. As a result of the time involved in this exercise, parliament receives the Community proposals only when they have been adopted already or will be very soon. As was observed above, the main reason for belated transposition[103] is of an administrative nature. On the one hand, the effects of proposed directives on national law are not taken into account in the negotiations; on the other, interministerial coordination is not sufficiently effective and disagreement between administrations leads to considerable blockages. Numerous min-

---

[103] On 30 June 2003, 84 directives had not been transposed within the prescribed period.

isterial circulars aim at improving this situation, for instance by drawing up a legal impact study for each proposed directive,[104] but these have been without result up to now. Two proposals of the Senate – to enable a parliamentary check of the transposition of directives and to organise a monthly meeting on this issue – were rejected by government, which instead installed a working group for improving transposition procedures. The suggestions this working group has put forward have not been given any follow-up until now. The delegation of the National Assembly dealing with EU affairs decided to publish an annual report on belated transposition of directives and the causes thereof.[105] As a result of a fairly recent circular of the Prime minister,[106] the Council of State may be called upon to give advice on all legal, essentially constitutional, questions that may occur regarding European acts that are being negotiated. Such an advice has been given in respect of the proposed European arrest warrant.

The **British** rapporteur observes that having a common glossary of autonomous expressions might assist in improving the quality and consistency of European legislation. There should be a lexicon of defined terms, terms defined throughout the directives, whatever the subject matter of the directive. If a term defined in one directive is adopted in the same sense in another, this should be explicitly stated.

2.2   The use of interpretation aids

In interpreting European legislation, what relevance is given to and what use is made of travaux préparatoires – both of European and national transposition legislation –, preambles, statements in the minutes of the Council, Commission documents drawn up subsequent to legislation or other documents? (questions 2.1.3-2.1.7 of the questionnaire)

2.2.1 *The approach in the case law of the ECJ*

In their report, Judges Puissochet and Timmermans give a fairly detailed account of the state of affairs as to the role played by various forms of *travaux préparatoires* and other documents in the interpretation of Community law by the ECJ.[107] They start by stating that, in respect of secondary Community law,

---

[104] See the circular of 9 November 1998 concerning the follow-up procedure of transposition of Community law directives into national law.

[105] See the report by Christian Philip, no. 1009 (2002-2003), op. cit., n. 66.

[106] Circular No. 4, 904/SG of 20 January 2003, not published.

[107] They also refer, in this respect, to Schønberg and Frick, *Finishing, refining, polishing: On the use of* travaux préparatoires *as an aid to the interpretation of Community legislation*, ELRev. 2003, p. 149 (170).

recourse to *travaux préparatoires* constitutes a significant interpretation method.[108] The case law shows that, in most cases, the Court makes use of *travaux préparatoires* with a view to confirming its interpretation of a Community law provision or to reject an opposite interpretation put before the Court. However, in some judgments, *travaux préparatoires* play a more decisive role and are invoked by the Court in order to establish the interpretation of the provision at issue. Next, they distinguish four types of *travaux préparatoires*.

The first category is the published *travaux préparatoires*, established by the Community institutions in the framework of the legislative procedure of the Community act to be interpreted. These are the *travaux préparatoires* the ECJ consults most frequently with a view to rejecting or confirming the interpretation of the provision at issue, for instance, proposals or amendments not retained in the final text or the explanatory memorandum adopted by the Commission.[109]

The second category concerns non-published documents, established by the Community institutions in the framework of the legislative procedure of the act to be interpreted, but which are not expressly provided for in the Treaty. Recourse to such documents – in particular to declarations made by one or more Member States, by the Council or by the Commission which are inserted in the minutes of the Council during the adoption of the act at issue – is only possible under certain conditions which aim at safeguarding of the principle of legal certainty. According to established case law, such a declaration cannot be taken into account in the interpretation of a secondary Community law provision if its contents are not in any way expressed in the text of this provision.[110] Furthermore, the Court has ruled that intentions expressed by Member States within the Council do not have a legal scope if they are not upheld in the legal provisions.[111] In the *Generics (UK)* case, however, the Court has refined this case law, by indicating that such a declaration, to the extent to which it aims at specifying a general notion, can be taken into account for the interpretation of such a provision.[112]

---

[108] Reference is made in this respect also to para. 4 of the Interinstitutional agreement on better law-making, OJ 2003, C 321/1, which provides that appropriate publication of *travaux préparatoires* has to be ensured.

[109] See Case C-133/00 *Bowden,* ECR [2001] I-7031, para. 42; Case C-363/01 *Flughafen Hannover-Langenhagen,* judgment of 16 October 2003, not yet reported, para. 50; Case C-245/01 *RTL Television,* judgment of 23 October 2003, not yet reported, para. 60; Case C-100/02 *Gerolsteiner Brunnen,* judgment of 7 January 2004, not yet reported, paras. 14-15.

[110] Case C-292/89 *Antonissen,* ECR [1991] I-745, para. 18; Case C-329/95 *VAG Sverige,* ECR [1997] I-2675, para. 23; Case C-104/01 *Libertel,* ECR [2003] I-3793, para. 25.

[111] Joined cases C-283/94, C-291/94, and C-292/94 *Denkavit & Others,* ECR [1996] I-5063, para. 29.

[112] Case C-368/96 *Generics (UK) & Others*, ECR [1998] I-7967, para. 27.

The third category encompasses the *travaux préparatoires* established by the Community institutions before the start of the legislative procedure of the act to be interpreted, such as resolutions of the Council and the EP or White and Green Papers. These are very little used as interpretation aids and it is also considered that recourse to such instruments should be had only carefully, as their influence on the final text of the regulation at issue is often difficult to establish.

The fourth category concerns the *travaux préparatoires* established within the framework of international organs or during treaty negotiations. The Court refers regularly to such *travaux préparatoires* of instruments of international public law, firstly, when the Court is directly competent to interpret the provisions of an international convention. It thus appears from numerous judgments that the Jenard and Schlösser reports sometimes play a significant role in the interpretation of the Brussels Convention of 1968.[113] Such *travaux préparatoires* may also play a role in the interpretation of primary or secondary Community law that derives from or is closely linked to provisions of an international convention.[114] Yet, a careful approach to *travaux préparatoires* of international public law instruments must be adopted when such use may not be appropriate given the particular context of the Community act to be interpreted.[115]

As regards documents adopted after the legislative procedure of the act to be interpreted, it is observed that these are sometimes invoked by the Court as an interpretation aid, even if these do not constitute *travaux préparatoires* in the strict sense of the word. Such documents include, *inter alia*, certain Commission guidelines, communications, or reports.[116] In the area of food safety, the Court also regularly refers to scientific studies as contextual interpretation

---

[113] See in particular Case C-412/98 *Group Josi,* ECR [2000] I-5925, paras. 35 and 74; Case C-256/00 *Besix,* ECR [2002] I-1699, para. 30; Case C-37/00 *Weber,* ECR [2002] I-2013, para. 56; Case C-80/00 *Italian Leather,* ECR [2002] I-4995, para. 48; Case C-271/00 *Baten,* ECR [2002] I-10489, para. 48.

[114] See, e.g., Case C-245/01 *RTL Television*, judgment of 23 October 2003, not yet reported, para. 63.

[115] See for an illustration of this the discussion in the report submitted by Judges Puissochet and Timmermans, of the Cases C-187/01 and C-385/01 *Gözütok and Brügge,* ECR [2003] I-1345 concerning the interpretation of Article 54 of the Convention for the application of the Schengen Agreement.

[116] See Case C-113/00 *Spain v. Commission,* ECR [2002] I-7601, para. 71; Case C-236/01 *Monsanto Agricoltura Italia*, judgment of 9 September 2003, not yet reported, para. 79; Case C-102/02 *Beuttenmüller*, judgment of 29 April 2004, not yet reported, para. 42, respectively.

elements.[117] However, so far, the Court has not accepted Green Papers for this purpose.[118]

2.2.2 *Transparency and* travaux préparatoires

In most Member States, some use is made of the available *travaux prépara-toires* and preambles, in particular in the case of serious interpretation problems or when the law is not clear. The preamble seems to play the most important role in this regard, but Commission documents too may sometimes be used for interpretation purposes. Statements in the Council minutes can be said to play a negligible role in this regard.[119] Overall, the national reports show wide agreement on the necessity of greater transparency of the European decision-making process and of greater availability of and easier access to the *travaux prépara-toires*, in order to facilitate and improve the transposition, application and interpretation of European law and of national transposition legislation.

Transparency is considered to mean that the main ideas behind the rules, the reasons why a specific clause is used or why a provision has been changed, etc., can be traced by those who have to apply the norms (**Austria**, **the Netherlands**). As such, it is also considered to improve the quality of the legislation itself (**Sweden**). The concrete suggestions that were made with a view to realising this will be discussed in Chapter 3, section 2. At the same time, some rapporteurs also underlined that the transparency of the European decision-making procedure has already considerably improved over the past few years (**Belgium**) and that one should not overestimate the relevance of the *travaux préparatoires*, in particular in view of the limited relevance the ECJ has attached to these (**Spain**, **Greece**, **the Netherlands**).

The **Austrian** rapporteur thinks that *travaux préparatoires* contribute to clarifying the meaning of clauses, by explaining the substance of the provision at stake, in particular when this has been changed in the legislative procedure. Detailed explanations concerning an amended proposal of the Commission are considered very helpful in this regard. Greater availability of systematic and complete *travaux préparatoires* would speed up the interpretation process and in many cases help to exclude one or the other possible hypothesis on the

---

[117] See, e.g., Case C-286/02 *Bellio F.lli*, judgment of 1 April 2004, not yet reported, paras. 42-43.

[118] Case C-154/00 *Commission v. Greece,* ECR [2002] I-3879, paras. 25-26; Case C-52/00 *Commission v. France,* ECR [2002] I-3827, para. 34.

[119] But cf., the Finnish preliminary reference Case C-233/97 *KappAhl Oy,* ECR [1998] I-8069, in which the question was put forward whether individual positions and a joint declaration adopted by the Member States in the course of the negotiations which led to the adoption of the Act of Accession, could be used for the purposes of interpreting a provision of that Act.

meaning of a clause. In one of the few cases in which the Administrative Court referred to *travaux préparatoires*, it held that a certain interpretation of EC law was not acceptable because it lacked confirmation in the *travaux prépara-toires*.[120] *Travaux préparatoires* of national legislation have also been used, in order to find out whether or not EC law had to be considered for the interpretation of the national legislation.[121]

The **Finnish** rapporteur also considers that, since legislation is a purposive activity, all information concerning the aims and objectives of those that drafted and decided on the provisions is potentially valuable as interpretative material. It may help to exclude certain interpretations or explain certain terminological choices in the act, etc. The fact that in the Finnish courts preparatory documents have been only of minor significance in interpreting European legislation is not attributable to a reluctance to do so, but to their limited availability, the general thought that they should not been given great importance, if any, and the absence of detailed statements of reasons. In interpreting national (transposition) legislation, Finnish courts give great importance to *travaux préparatoires* and are thus familiar with using preparatory works as a source of interpretation.

In **Luxemburg**, recourse to *travaux préparatoires* is only being had in the case the scope, aim or meaning of a text is not clear. *Travaux préparatoires* may then be useful with a view to establishing the aim and a full understanding of the scope of the European text at issue. Until now, the case has not presented itself yet. Examples of the use of *travaux préparatoires* of national transposition legislation are not known either, but such a use is considered possible.

The **Dutch** rapporteur considers that *travaux préparatoires* may be particularly useful with a view to the transposition of European legislation in the national legal order since there is no case law yet on a particular issue. In implementation it is important that an arguable approach is taken and the drafting history of an act provides a useful yardstick for this. At the judicial level, use of the European *travaux préparatoires* occurs foremost when a directive provision raises questions and has, for instance, been introduced in the course of the legislative process. When the interpretation of a European norm itself is at stake, no use is made of the *travaux préparatoires* of national transposition legislation. This occurs only when the legislation itself is at issue, concerning for example the question whether a reference provision is of a static or a dynamic nature.[122]

---

[120] Decision 98/17/0100 of 30 August 1999.

[121] E.g., decisions of 18 March 2002, 99/17/0136, of 26 June 2000, 99/17/0450, of 30 August 1999, 98/17/0100, and of 21 December 1998, 96/17/0079.

[122] Cf., the judgment of 10 April 2003 in Case 2000050000/1 (RTL) concerning reference to Directive 89/552/EEC. On implementation by static and dynamic referral, see section 1.3.

At the **Danish** jurisdictional level, use may be made of *travaux prépara-toires*, which is illustrated by the fact that the Supreme Court[123] made use of the Schlösser Report in a case concerning the interpretation of Article 16, sub-section 1, of the Convention of 27 September 1968 on jurisdiction and the enforcement of judgments in civil and commercial matters (the Brussels Con-vention).[124] When interpreting national transposition legislation, reference may be made to *travaux préparatoires* of the Danish legislation.[125]

In **Germany**, recourse is only had to explanatory documents in the case that the national norm that aims at transposing European law produces incoherent results. The judge will try to find an interpretation that respects both the Euro-pean and the national norm, giving priority to the European norm in the case they are not compatible. The explanatory texts are indispensable for doing so, and the national court will use them with a view to avoiding reference of preli-minary questions. The only problem is the limited availability of these docu-ments. National *travaux préparatoires* may also prove to be useful, but they are considered an auxiliary instrument inferior to the text itself, which has to be interpreted literally and in its context while respecting the primacy of European law. More generally, it is considered that the historical interpretation method is an option only in the case that neither the text nor the context permits appropriate conclusions. In this respect, mention is made of the fact that ambiguity of the text is often the result of compromise or is deliberate, leaving some margin of discre-tion to the national legislatures. Furthermore, in some cases the use of *travaux préparatoires* may even render the uniform application of European law more difficult, as each Member State might invoke its particular notion of the text.

The **Swedish** rapporteur also points to the fact that it is not always possible to find a consistent will behind a European legal act, given its compromising nature. In the Swedish legal tradition, *travaux préparatoires* play an important role in the interpretation of unclear laws. If preparatory works are easily acces-sible to all, the knowledge that they will be used to clarify uncertainties in-creases legal certainty. Since European *travaux préparatoires* are scarce, they are not considered an important factor for interpretation. The national *travaux préparatoires* are not used to ascertain the meaning of the European rule but are considered to be useful for determining whether the solution made by the na-tional legislature is in conformity with the European rule or not.

---

[123] U 2001, p. 2524.

[124] OJ 1979, C 59/71.

[125] For instance, the Eastern High Court referred to the *travaux préparatoires* of the Danish employment contract law which implemented Directive 91/533/EEC on an employer's obliga-tion to inform employees of the conditions applicable to the contract or employment relationship, when assessing whether the law was applicable in the case at hand; U 2003, p. 932.

The **Belgian** rapporteur notes that it is rather exceptional that the advice of the legislative department of the Council of State and the judgments of its administrative department show that *travaux préparatoires* were used with a view to interpreting European directives, except for preambles (see below). In rare cases, reference may be made to preparatory documents such as a Commission proposal or its explanatory memorandum.[126] Nevertheless, the magistrates of the Council of State may have recourse to the preparatory documents that are available through the Internet, for instance, with a view to verifying whether they confirm the interpretation that ensues from the legislative text itself. In such cases, no reference may be made to *travaux préparatoires* in the advice or judgment. National *travaux préparatoires* of implementing legislation are used in the same way as *travaux préparatoires* of other domestic law.

According to the **British** rapporteur, English courts will sometimes have regard to the *travaux préparatoires* of Community instruments in circumstances where they believe that the ECJ would itself do so.[127] Such *travaux préparatoires* as are already available are occasionally useful in interpreting Community instruments or, as in case C-453/03,[128] assessing the strength of a challenge of validity. Yet, it is suspected that the use of *travaux préparatoires* will always remain a tool whose uses are limited, particularly with the spread of the co-decision procedure, which makes it difficult to assume that views expressed by either the Commission, the Council, or the Parliament necessarily expresses the will of the Community legislature. The rapporteur further observes that, although there may be good political reasons for greater transparency in the legislative process, it may be doubted that making a verbatim record of Council debates will be of significant assistance in interpreting Community instruments. The experience of English courts is that recourse to national parliamentary debates rarely discloses sufficiently clear and unambiguous evidence of the legislative intent behind a provision whose interpretation is disputed. It would be a surprise if the outcome were much different where Community instruments are concerned. As regards the use of *travaux préparatoires* of national implementing legislation, the English courts may look at pre-legislative materials (e.g., White Papers) and at explanatory notes. Reference may also be made to statements made in parliament for the purposes of construing a statutory provision where (a) the legislation is ambiguous or obscure, or leads to an absurdity, (b) the material relied on consists of statements by a minister or other promotor of the Bill (together with material necessary to understand such statements and

---

[126] See, e.g., C.E. (section d'administration), *Acke & Others*, No. 97.221 of 28 June 2001.
[127] See, e.g., the order for reference of the High Court in Case C-453/03 R *(ABNA) v. S./S Health*, OJ 2004, C 7/22.
[128] Case C-453/03 R *(ABNA) v. S./S Health*, still pending.

their effect), and (c) the effect of such statements is clear. Laws passed in order to give effect to Community obligations are no exception to these principles. The courts are mindful, however, that whatever the actual intention of the legislature, they must so far as possible interpret national implementing legislation in accordance with the European legislation that it implements. Where implementation legislation is concerned, therefore, the need for an interpretation compliant with Community law overrides the need to discern what the national legislature actually intended.

In **Italy**, *travaux préparatoires* are used when interpretation difficulties present themselves pursuant to, for example, contradicting national judgments or in relation to judgments in other Member States. In such cases, it may be useful to have recourse to Commission documents. Yet, only rarely recourse will be had to the *travaux préparatoires* of the national transposition legislation, as it is considered more appropriate to rely on the original European text itself and perhaps to examine other language versions.

Quite a different approach is followed in **Portugal**, where the tendency of the administration and the national courts is to interpret national transposition legislation in conformity with national laws, assuming that the national legislature has done a good job in transposing European legislation. In that framework, recourse may also be had to the *travaux préparatoires* thereof. Usually, it is only pursuant to a complaint of one of the parties alleging that European law has not been respected that it is examined whether the transposition into national law has been satisfactory. In such a case, courts sometimes study the text of the directive, the *travaux préparatoires*, the preamble or other explanatory texts.

The **Greek** Council of State often has recourse to *travaux préparatoires* of national laws, in particular the explanatory memorandum, the scientific report of the House of Representatives and the parliamentary debates. Although they are certainly an important source of information, their relevance should not be overestimated since judges often resort to interpretation methods that depart from a literal, textual interpretation and the will of the legislature, and give preference to systematic and teleological interpretation. As regards European legislation, it is pointed to its difficult accessibility, the limited significance of these documents in the interpretation process and the risks that go along with a plethora of information.

The **Spanish** view differs from those expressed above in the sense that it is not considered certain that greater transparency of the legislative process will entail better implementation and interpretation of European legislation. In particular, it is considered that all acts that may have an influence on interpretation are already being published in the *Official Journal*, with the exclusion of declarations of the Council, Commission or Member States issued during Council meetings, which are recorded in the minutes and in the monthly compilations drawn up by the Secretariat-General of the Council.[129] However, given the limited relevance which may be attached to these declarations as a result of the ECJ's case law (merely confirming an interpretation which already ensues from other elements)[130] and the danger that publication in the *OJ* may actually lead national organs to award them a normative value which they do not have, changes are not deemed advisable in this regard. It is further noted that in principle *travaux préparatoires* are not used.

In the same line of thinking, the **Belgian** rapporteur concludes in particular that the degree of transparency of European legislation that results from Article 207(3) EC and the Council's Rules of Procedure[131] seems to strike the right balance between the requirements of efficacy and transparency. The public nature of preparatory European documents is considered at least equivalent to that of similar national documents. Furthermore, Article 49(2) of the draft Constitutional Treaty provides that not only the EP but also the deliberations of the Council on legislative proposals will be public. Remaining difficulties relate in particular to the availability of internal documents of working groups, at the stage of both the preparation of legislative acts and of their implementation.

In **France**, *travaux préparatoires* are used and, even though their availability through devices such as Prelex remains limited, the rapporteur is also of the opinion that the European decision-making process meets the transparency requirements of a democratic legal system. Nonetheless, increasing transparency could benefit the application of European legislation. The administrative judge considers that recourse to parliamentary *travaux préparatoires* is only acceptable in the case a text is ambiguous, which can be said to apply also to European legislation. Since directives are often considered to be very technical and difficult to understand, it seems that *travaux préparatoires* are often used. A problem is, however, that the main interpretation difficulties occur in respect of acts that have been modified in the Council, on which *travaux préparatoires* are often lacking. Moreover, the national judge has little room to manoeuvre since in the case of serious interpretation difficulties he may have to ask preliminary questions. Since the *travaux préparatoires* of national legislation are for French courts one of the major means for teleological interpretation, the same can be said to go for national transposition legislation.[132]

---

[129] Since the adoption by the Council of the Code of Conduct on the publishing of Council minutes and statements in the minutes, 2 October 1995.

[130] See, e.g., Case 136/78 *Auer,* ECR [1979] 437 and Case C-292/89 *Antonissen,* ECR [1991] I-505.

[131] Contained in Council Decision 2002/682/EC, OJ 2002, L 230/7.

[132] See, e.g., Report No. 322 (1996-1997) by senator Balarello.

2.2.3 *Preamble*

In most Member States, the preamble is considered a very important aid for the interpretation of European law, as it is deemed to be of the same legislative quality as the text it precedes and delimits the framework of interpretation (**Germany**); it is considered an integral part of the piece of legislation (**Sweden**); it is seen as an element that sheds light on the reasons behind and the aim of a particular provision (**Italy, Germany, Luxemburg**); it serves as an explanatory memorandum (**Greece**); frequently recourse is taken to preambles in jurisdiction (**the Netherlands**).[133] The **Danish** Supreme Court determined the scope of Directive 85/337/EEC on environmental impact assessment by making specific reference to its preamble in a case in which Greenpeace claimed that the Minister of Traffic had violated this directive.[134] The **Spanish** Supreme Court judges also look quite frequently to the preambles of European acts, with a view to establishing their interpretation.[135]

The **British** courts seek to interpret Community legislation in accordance with the preamble to the extent that the ECJ does so.[136] Although it has no exact equivalent in UK legislation, the preamble is welcomed as a helpful and accessible guide to the intention of the Community legislature. The **Belgian** Council of State may refer to the preamble when the interpretation cannot be deduced from the text and logic of the directive itself.[137] The legislative department of the Council of State quite often refers to the preamble of directives, in particular with a view to supporting an interpretation that was already founded on other considerations.[138] Sometimes, however, the reference to the preamble is at the heart of the motivation of an advice.[139] The administrative section may also refer to the preamble to support an interpretation ensuing already from the

---

[133] Cf., the judgment of the Administrative Jurisdiction Division of the Council of State of 10 April 2001, No. 2000050000/1 (RTL), AB 2002, 5. This case concerned the interpretation of the amendment of Art. 2 of Directive 89/552/EEC (Television without frontiers) in Directive 97/36/EC, which concerns the delimitation of supervisory competences of the Member States.

[134] U 1995, p. 634.

[135] Cf., its judgments of 18 October 2002 (concerning Regulation 404/1993), 12 December 2002, 18 March 2003 (concerning Regulation 2677/1985), 21 March 2003 (concerning Directive 84/253) and 12 June 2003.

[136] Case C-404/97 *Commission v. Portugal* ECR [2000] I-4897, para. 41.

[137] See, e.g., C.E. (section d'administration), *Mouvement contre le racisme, l'antisémitisme et la xénophobie (MRAX)*, 23 November 1999, No. 83.584.

[138] See Advice Nos. 34.361/4 of 24 February 2003; 19.705/8 of 23 May and 20 November 1990; 19.732/8 of 13 March 1990; 20.204/8 of 6 November 1990.

[139] Advice No. 19.704/VR/8 of 23 May and 9 July 1990.

directive[140] or to help establish an interpretation following from a judgment by the CFI.[141] However, the preamble is not considered a sufficient basis for the Council of State to solve an interpretation problem by itself; it will ask the ECJ, while providing the Court with the elements considered useful for interpretation, including the preamble.

Rather in contrast with these views, the **Finnish** rapporteur observes that, in general, it is felt that the legal status and the importance of the preamble remain somewhat unclear – between a legal rule and an explanatory memorandum – which makes it difficult to understand. As a result, the preamble has not been given great relevance in interpretation, although there are some examples where the courts have referred to it. The **Austrian** Administrative Court every now and then tries to draw conclusions from the preamble, which, however, seldom allows the deduction of a precise answer to a specific question because it is of a too general nature.[142] In **France** too, this use seems very limited.[143]

2.2.4 *Statements in the minutes of the Council*

Statements in the minutes of the Council are not frequently used for interpretation purposes. Some rapporteurs observe that there is no recorded use (**Portugal, Belgium, Sweden, the Netherlands**), that such use would not be very helpful (**France**) or that reference may be made to such statements if they are presented to the court (**Denmark**). The **German** rapporteur points to the fact that these statements are usually inaccessible for national courts, that there is a linguistic problem and that their use is limited because they may reflect the position of only one Member State and not the objective will of the legislature. The **Greek** Council of State takes a position close to that taken by the ECJ in the *Antonissen* case. Although they may be considered to form part of the *travaux préparatoires*, no statement of a Member State issued during the adoption procedure of a European act can affect its application. Likewise, a declaration cannot be used for the interpretation of a directive if the contents itself of such a declaration has not been in any way expressed in the directive. The **British** rapporteur states that two preliminary rulings on references from English courts are thought to have defined the circumstances in which reference may be made

---

[140] E.g., C.E. (section d'administration), a.s.b.l. *Ligue belge pour la protection des oiseaux*, No. 38.422, 7 January 1992.

[141] C.E. (section d'administration), *Dufrasne Métaux*, No. 94.080, 16 March 2001.

[142] E.g., decisions of 28 January 2002, 99/17/0407 and of 20 December 1999, 99/17/0375.

[143] For an example, see, however, Report No. 348 (1994-1995) by senator Hugot, concerning the bill implementing Directive 93/7.

to statements in the minutes of the Council of Ministers.[144] The English courts follow that guidance.

2.2.5 *Commission documents*

Generally speaking, it appears that most Member States do not exclude the use of Commission documents that have been adopted at a later stage than the legislation itself, but that usually they are not given so much weight.

It is thus observed that the court will make use of such documents if it has knowledge of them, but that one cannot speak of an established routine in this regard (**Germany**) and that they are a source of information amongst other sources but do not in any way bind the national judge (**Greece**, **Luxemburg**). The **Danish** rapporteur observes that it is for the court to decide what weight to attach to such a source of interpretation, but that, unlike *travaux préparatoires*, they are not regarded as an original source of law. The **Swedish** rapporteur makes a similar observation, stating further that to his knowledge the Supreme Administrative Court has never relied on such documents. In **Luxemburg**, it has occurred that documentation of the Commission concerning its position in an infringement proceeding was produced before the Court and that this has been admitted to the file of the case. In **the Netherlands**, interpretative Commission notices are taken into consideration only when the Commission has discretionary powers, for instance as regards the determination of protected areas on the basis of Directive 92/43/EEC. Annual Commission reports and answers from the Commission to questions of the EP may also contain useful background information.

Finnish courts will not systematically search for or study Commission documents, such as notices or guides. However, if the case is important or difficult from the point of view of European law, all available material will be acquired *ex officio* if it is not produced by the parties. Commission documents may then give factual information which is useful for interpretation, but they are not given any more qualified importance unless this results from the status of the document itself. In competition law cases, Commission documents have had particular significance. The same applies to the Interpretation Manual of European Union Habitats[145] so far as the Natura 2000 cases are concerned. According to the **Austrian** rapporteur, such Commission documents may support the arguments leading to the conclusion that there is no room for doubt as to how a European law provision should be interpreted, referring to a decision of the

---

[144] Case C-292/89 *Antonissen,* ECR [1991] I-745 and Case C-368/96 *Generics,* ECR [1998] I-7967.
[145] Version EUR 15, of 24 April 1996.

Administrative Court in which it abstained from referring preliminary questions to the ECJ as several of its assumptions were shared by Commission documents.[146] In rather exceptional cases, it may occur that the **Belgian** Council of State has recourse to Commission documents with a view to confirming its interpretation of a European text. This has been the case, for instance, in respect of the Commission vademecum on the general system of recognition of professional qualifications[147] and its Guide on the conservation of natural habitats and of wild fauna and flora.[148] It also occurs that the administrative section of the Council of State uses Commission documents as a foundation for a certain interpretation. It has done this, for instance, in respect of the Commission communication of 23 July 1997 relating to environmental taxes and charges in the single market.[149] The Council of State also refers to Commission decisions in areas in which the Commission has a proper decision-making power, such as in the area of state aid. In **Spain**, recourse is had in particular to Commission communications, such as those adopted in the area of competition law. The **French** rapporteur found only one example of a State Councillor referring to a Commission report.[150] The national legislature seems to make more use thereof, as parliamentary documents show references to Commission acts and contacts with the Commission in order to clarify notions contained in directives.

In **Portugal**, courts refuse to have recourse to such Commission documents, considering that if they were to be part of the legislative text there would be no use in issuing them and if they go beyond the legislative text, they are not binding. The **British** rapporteur also observes that it is difficult to see how such documents could be an admissible aid to the interpretation of prior legislation. However, if national authorities have taken a position that is inconsistent with such a Commission document, the divergence might be a factor in favour of requesting a preliminary ruling under Article 234 EC.[151]

2.3 Recourse to different language versions

Are different language versions used in interpreting legislation? Are the different language versions regarded as a threat to correct and uniform interpreta-

---

[146] Decision of 20 March 2003, 2000/17/0084.

[147] Advice No. 30.239 of 22 November 2000.

[148] Advice Nos. 30.537 to 30.541.

[149] OJ 1997, C 224/6. C.E. (section d'administration), *Fédération des exportateurs de vins et spiritueux de France*, No. 126.158, 8 December 2003. For another example, see C.E. (section d'administration), *Wellens & others*, 4 September 1998, No. 75.678.

[150] Conclusions on CE 8/3 SSR, 5 June 2002, *Société Havas interactive*, No. 232392.

[151] This happened in Case C-36/03 *R (APS) v. Licensing Authority*, OJ 2003, C 83/7, still pending.

tion of European law or do they contribute to this? (question 2.1.8 of the questionnaire)

2.3.1 *Approach of the ECJ in the case of linguistic divergences*

Judges Puissochet and Timmermans have briefly summarised, in their report, the way in which the ECJ deals with the different language versions in its case law and what role they are assigned in its interpretation of Community law. They state that, according to established case law, the different language versions of a Community text have to be interpreted uniformly and in the case of divergences between these versions, the provision at issue must be interpreted in the light of the general approach and objective of the text of which it forms part. Recent case law confirms this, also making it clear that the number of people who use a certain language or the fact that the majority of the language versions supports a certain interpretation are in principle no relevant factors.[152] The *Givane* judgment also makes clear that, before having recourse to the 'context' of the provision to be interpreted, i.e., its spirit and its objective, the Court examines whether the problem can be resolved by way of a literal interpretation. Literal interpretation thus precedes teleological interpretation, and the comparison of different language versions constitutes one of the methods of literal interpretation. The Court's judgment in the *RTL Television* case illustrates this. In this case, the Court first examined whether the wording of the directive, the relevant documents for the interpretation thereof (*travaux préparatoires*), the usual meaning, and a comparison of the language versions allowed for the interpretation of the notions of 'films made for television' and of 'series' at issue in Article 11, paragraph 3 of the Television without Frontiers Directive.[153] Yet, it is possible that even a teleological interpretation does not help to resolve a divergence between different language versions, as, for instance, the *Privat-Molkerei Borgmann* case makes clear.[154]

2.3.2 *National approaches*

It appears that, as a rule, national courts only use the national language version of European legislation and may have recourse to other language versions only in order to solve serious interpretation problems. Overall, it seems that compar-

---

[152] See Case C-257/00 *Givane & Others,* ECR [2003] I-345, para. 40; Case C-1/02 *Privat-Molkerei Borgmann*, judgment of 1 April 2004, not yet reported, para. 25; Case C-341/01 *Plato Plastik*, judgment of 29 April 2004, not yet reported, para. 64.

[153] Case C-245/01 *RTL Television,* judgment of 23 October 2003, not yet reported.

[154] Case C-1/02 *Privat-Molkerei Borgmann*, judgment of 1 April 2004, not yet reported.

ison of language versions serves in particular the elimination of interpretation problems in practice. In **Sweden**, the different language versions are thus deemed very useful for determining the correct interpretation of a particular concept and for establishing whether the expression used in the national language version is the proper one. Yet, some rapporteurs consider themselves not in a position to indicate whether different language versions are a threat to the correct interpretation of European law or not (**Denmark**) or have no knowledge of an evaluation of the possible benefits and disadvantages thereof (**Portugal**). The **Finnish** rapporteur observes that given the limited number of situations in which the interpretation difficulty is mainly to be attributed to differences in language versions, it is difficult to estimate the global impact of these differences.

The foregoing is not to say that the national courts have a common approach to recourse to other language versions. In some states the use of language versions other than the national ones or a comparison thereof seems thus more or less excluded (**Luxemburg**) or is unknown (**Portugal**). **Spanish** courts only consider other language versions when one of the parties draws attention to differences between them or when the court itself observes a 'strange' element. In **Belgium**, the European provisions are considered in the language of the proceedings that are taking place. Only when an interpretation problem poses itself in this language version or when the attention of the Council of State is drawn specifically to divergences between different language versions of a directive will it consider other language versions. These are usually the versions of the other national languages of Belgium, and English. These divergences are considered to be a source of interpretation problems in themselves. According to the rapporteur, the Council follows the method recommended by the ECJ, which is that, in the case of diverging language versions, the true purpose and aim pursued by its author have to be taken into account.[155]

In more Member States, recourse to other language versions appears to be common. In **Germany**, recourse may thus be had to other language versions already at the transposition stage, in the case that the final legislative text does not correspond to the results of previous negotiations in the working languages. At the judicial level, this use is limited because of the limited knowledge of judges of other languages. Yet, there are some examples of such a comparison.[156] The **Greek** Council of State often has recourse to the French, English, German and Italian language versions, which are considered to contribute to solving interpretation problems. The **Austrian** Administrative Court, too, fre-

---

[155] Advice No. 36.126/4 of 27 November 2003.

[156] Case decided by the Federal Administrative Court, regarding the interpretation of Decision 1/80 adopted by the Association Council created by the EEC – Turkey Association Agreement, involving comparison of the German, French and English versions.

quently uses the French and English versions with a view to confirming one or another possible interpretation of a term or clause,[157] and hence the existence of different language versions is not regarded as a threat to the uniform interpretation and application of European law. In **Finland**, comparison is usually limited to the three EU languages most often used and to Danish, Swedish and Finnish. Comparison often helps to clarify an ambiguous provision. If the text in one language is clear, the other languages are not necessarily studied, but if this is done, the clear provision in one language version may actually become obscure. In **the Netherlands**, the English, French and German language versions may be compared to the Dutch one. In some cases, this has elucidated the meaning of a particular provision, for instance whether the provision *met name* [particularly] in Article 5(d) of Directive 79/409/EEC was intended as a limitation or not. In isolated cases, however, comparison may complicate existing questions, which occurred for instance in respect of Directive 89/552/EEC concerning the term *televisie-omroep* [television broadcasting]. In other cases, comparison may not provide a solution.[158]

The **British** rapporteur observes that the desirability of considering different language versions in cases of ambiguity or doubt has often been stressed by English judges. Lord Denning in *Bulmer v. Bollinger* (1974) thus urged the English courts to consider all the authentic texts of a Community provision. Advocate-General Warner stated in 1986 that it is generally unwise to look at the text of a Community measure in one language only. The possibility of divergences between language versions is treated as a factor in favour of a case being referred to the ECJ under Article 234 EC. Where wider-ranging submissions are to be made on different language versions, the Court of Appeal has held that the parties should seek to agree in advance on the meaning of the versions in question; that submissions based on disputed translations of foreign-language texts are unlikely to be productive; but that if such submissions are pursued, it should be on the basis of evidence from translators, followed if necessary by cross-examination.[159]

---

[157] E.g., decisions of 23 October 2000, 2000/17/0058, of 17 December 2002, 2002/17/0047, of 21 December 2001, 99/19/0185, and of 4 September 2003, 2003/17/0094.

[158] Cf., Case C-72/95 *Kraaijeveld*, ECR [1996] I-5403, in which the meaning of 'canalization and flood-relief works' was at issue, contained in Directive 85/337/EEC of 27 June 1985 on the assessment of the effects of certain public and private projects on the environment.

[159] See Case *R v. CCE ex parte EMU Tabac* [1997] EuLR 153.

2.4   Recourse to consistent interpretation and reliance on direct effect

To what extent are interpretations in conformity with directives or Community law used in interpreting national legislation implementing European legislation? (question 2.1.2 of the questionnaire)

Virtually all national reports point to consistent interpretation as being the – very important – tool for the national court to solve interpretation problems, even though the national court may not always state this explicitly. Reliance on direct effect (and the issue of the primacy of European law as such) appears to play a less prominent role in this regard (**Finland, Greece, the Netherlands**).

In **Belgium**, it is a well-established rule that a law has to be interpreted in conformity with higher norms. The Court of Cassation[160] and the legislative and administrative departments of the Council of State clearly apply this rule also as regards Community law.[161] The **Luxemburg** rapporteur observes that national courts take the primacy of European law as the point of departure and that, if need be, they will try to interpret national law in conformity with it. The same goes for **Denmark**, where this approach fits in with the general principle according to which Danish legislation giving rise to doubts of interpretation must be interpreted in a manner which is best suited to bring it into harmony with Denmark's international obligations.[162] In **France**, consistent interpretation is accepted as regards national transposition legislation and also in respect of national laws that touch upon matters covered by European rules.[163]

Similarly, in **Finland**, with some rare exceptions, questions related to the relationship between European law and national law are solved through consistent interpretation. Only in two cases concerning indirect taxation, the Supreme Administrative Court clearly gave precedence to European law instead of conflicting national law. The preparedness to rely on consistent interpretation can partly be explained by the fact that since the Constitution does not give a special hierarchical status to international agreements, the Finnish courts are used to interpret national legislation in conformity with Finland's international obli-

---

[160] Cass., 2 December 1996, *Pas.*, 1996, I, p. 1205.

[161] See, e.g., Advice No. 33.182/2 of 29 April 2002.

[162] This is illustrated by a case concerning the repacking of parallel-imported pharmaceutical products, in which the Supreme Court interpreted Section 6, para. 2, of the Danish trademark law in accordance with Art. 7 of the First Council Directive 89/104/EEC on the approximation of the laws of the Member States relating to trademarks; U 2003, p. 1826.

[163] E.g., CE 20 October 2000, *Cambon*, No. 204129, p. 454; CE 8/3 SSR, 5 June 2002, *Société Havas interactive*, No. 232392; CE 6/4 SSR, 8 December 2000, *Commune de Breil-sur-Roya*, No. 204756, p. 582 and CE 6/4 SSR, 30 July 2003, *Association 'avenir de la langue française'*, No. 245076.

gations, which has in fact become established legal practice in the national courts. So, in the case of a conflict between an international norm and a national norm, the international norm does not have primacy as a matter of principle.

The **Spanish** rapporteur underlines that the national judicial and administrative organs have no difficulty in assuming the primacy and direct effect of secondary European law and that the Supreme Court has held that national implementing legislation has to be interpreted in conformity with the terms of the underlying directive.[164] Consistent interpretation also occurs in respect of national laws adopted prior to a European directive.[165] Furthermore, third-pillar framework decisions have been used to interpret the Penal Code, not only before the deadline for transposition had expired,[166] but also even when only proposed.[167]

In **Germany**, European legislation is said to enjoy the primacy of application, not legally but in practice. When a national provision is not in accordance with a European provision, a court will try to find an interpretation of the national norm that conforms to the European one. Yet, the German rapporteur also raises more fundamentally the issue of the limits to this obligation, by pointing to the fact that the Federal Administrative Court has put aside the hypothesis that consequences have to be attached to directives before the deadline for implementation has passed, even if it is clear that the legislature will not succeed in transposing the directive in time and that the directive may then have direct effect.[168] The rapporteur is aware of other views in legal doctrine, according to which interpretation in conformity with the directive imposes itself already before the deadline has passed. Yet, in the aforementioned Court judgment a limit has been found to lie in the principle of legal certainty. The obligation has to be fulfilled only at the moment the deadline passes and the Member State may profit from this until the last moment. Until then, its room to manoeuvre is not yet definitively limited. In this regard, the situation is deemed similar to that of modification of national law independently of a European law obligation, which will only obtain the status of law from the moment

---

[164] Judgment of 16 October 1995. E.g., in its ruling of 21 May 2003, it interpreted national Law 19/1996 in the light of Directive 84/253 of 10 April 1984 based on Art. 54 (3) (g) of the Treaty on the approval of persons responsible for carrying out the statutory audits of accounting documents.

[165] Cf., the judgment of the Supreme Court of 12 December 2002, concerning Directive 98/59 of 20 July 1998 on the approximation of the laws of the Member States relating to collective redundancies.

[166] Cf., the judgment of the Supreme Court of 8 July 2002, concerning the Framework Decision on the fight against fraud.

[167] Cf., the judgment of the Supreme Court of 26 February 2002.

[168] BverwG 4 NB21.92 – NVwZ 1992, 1093, order of 5 June 1992.

of its entry into force. It is also pointed to the fact that consistent interpretation may not lead to a *contra legem* interpretation of the national law. These limits do not impose themselves in the case that a European law provision has direct effect, in which case the internal rules cannot oppose themselves to this. Consistent interpretation is considered the only way of 'harmonising' the European law and the national law in the case that direct effect is lacking and it may lead to favourable though also unfavourable outcomes for the interested party.

Although the **Austrian** Administrative Court has frequent recourse to the method of consistent interpretation,[169] problems persist in its relation to the doctrine of direct effect; among other things, can the result of consistent interpretation really be that in fact the effect of direct application is achieved? Furthermore, the Administrative Court also held that consistent interpretation must not lead to going beyond the meaning of the wording of the national law.[170]

The **English** courts and tribunals are well aware that 'so far as possible', they must interpret national implementing legislation in accordance with the European legislation that it implements, and with Community law in general. They are also aware that directly effective provisions of Community law must be given precedence over inconsistent national provisions. For these reasons, the courts will frequently take as their starting-point the terms of the directive rather than (to the extent that it may be different) the terms of the national implementing legislation.

As regards **Portugal**, see section 2.2.

2.5   Recourse to the preliminary rulings procedure

> *To what extent do not so much legal but policy considerations – such as delay, wishes of the parties, etc. – affect the use of the preliminary procedure? Is the aim of the preliminary rulings procedure considered to be foremost the protection of the general interest of uniform application of European law or that of the individual's interest of legal protection?* (questions 2.2.1-2.2.2 of the questionnaire)

2.5.1 *Use*

Not only legal considerations – based on the terms of Article 234 EC and the *CILFIT* criteria – determine the decision to refer preliminary questions to the

---

[169] E.g., Decision 99/10/0159 of 27 June 2002, concerning Directive 92/43/EEC and Decision 98/10/0250 of 22 March 1999 concerning the Austrian Law on Foodstuffs. Cf., the decision of 20 November 2002, 2001/17/0180 for an example of direct application of European law.

[170] Decision 95/10/0108 of 23 October 1995.

ECJ, but also a number of policy considerations may play a role in this respect. Yet, the relevance thereof appears to differ from one Member State to another. Some states (such as **Italy**, **Portugal**, **Greece**, **the UK** and **Austria**) seem to apply the legal criteria imposed by Article 234 EC and the *CILFIT* judgment more strictly than others, which take policy considerations into account as well. These concern, *inter alia*, the delay of the proceedings (e.g., **Spain**, **Denmark**, **Finland**), the consequences of a judgment in intra-EU relations (**the Netherlands**, **France**), the fact that a similar question has been put forward by a judge from another Member State or that there are similar cases pending at the same time (**Finland**), the relevance of the answer to a question for other cases; if the interest is strong and the case suitable, questions will be posed more readily (**the Netherlands**). If it is expected that questions will arise in many cases, posing preliminary questions will be postponed until the scope of the problem is clear (**the Netherlands**). The **Italian** Supreme Court will consider a preliminary reference necessary in the case that the interpretation of a European law provision given by a lower judge differs from that which higher courts intend to follow.

As regards the issue of delay of proceedings, the **Danish** rapporteur considers that the opinions of the parties and the urgency of the matter will be of importance. Thus, in a criminal case concerning the violation of national provisions of indirect taxation, the Supreme Court did not refer the case in order to avoid prolongation of proceedings, despite the fact that the case involved questions regarding Article 95 EC requiring a preliminary ruling. Instead, the defendant was acquitted.[171] The **German** rapporteur thinks that it is not excluded that delay of proceedings may affect the decision to refer, but this is not considered to be of significant influence since the number of preliminary references actually gives proof of the contrary. According to the **Swedish** rapporteur, the time needed for a preliminary ruling is a serious problem and it can be argued that the national court ruling based on it, will come too late to be in conformity with Article 6 of the European Convention of Human Rights. For a court whose main task is to give rulings which have effect of precedent, it is sometimes inevitable, however, that the interest of a correct ruling has priority over the interest of a rapid handling of the case. The parties are heard both on the question whether a preliminary ruling should be requested and on how the question should be formulated. Their opinions are considered but not given decisive importance.

The **Finnish** Supreme Administrative Court also considers that the wishes of the parties or the fact that many similar cases are pending may have some influ-

---

[171] U 1994, p. 86.

ence on the decision to refer, but the Court also actively takes up *ex officio* European law points. Finnish legislation provides that sometimes the case has to be handled urgently and at other times the legal protection of the individual may require an urgent solution of the case. So far, however, this has not occurred with respect to the use of the preliminary procedure. The problem of the effects that a pending preliminary reference made by another court may have on cases before the Supreme Administrative Court presented itself in connection with the so-called Natura 2000 cases (see section 1.4). More than 1,200 appeals against the government decision establishing the lists of protected areas were pending before the Supreme Administrative Court when a British court referred a preliminary question on the interpretation of the Habitat Directive. Relying on the preliminary ruling issued by the ECJ on a similar interpretative question in the context of the Bird Directive, it was deemed possible to make the final decisions without waiting for the ECJ's judgment.

The **Portuguese** rapporteur is not aware of any policy considerations that may have led to the use of the preliminary procedure, even though parties may have suggested referring questions with a view to delaying proceedings. It is the judge who decides whether to refer or not and although the Portuguese courts make a modest use of the preliminary procedure, it is deemed sufficient and effective. Similarly, in **Luxemburg** parties may suggest to refer or not to refer questions, but it is the court that decides on this. The **Greek** rapporteur also observes that it was not possible to establish that the preliminary procedure was used for delaying purposes. Generally speaking, the Council of State conforms to the *CILFIT* criteria. However, in some cases the court has been too restrictive in its use of the preliminary procedure, which is illustrated by a series of cases in which the compatibility of Directive 89/48/EEC concerning the mutual recognition of diplomas with some provisions of the Constitution was at stake. Notwithstanding the opinion of a number of members of the Council of State that there was no question of *acte clair* in these cases, the Council decided that there was, and that thus there was no need to refer questions. The same occurred in another series of cases concerning some big public projects and whether a national provision was in conformity with Article 1(5) of Directive 85/337/EEC.

The **British** rapporteur states that, in the English jurisdiction, it is only legal, and not policy, considerations which affect the decisions to request the ECJ for a preliminary ruling. The need for a uniform interpretation of the directives throughout the Community is borne in mind and the question is asked whether the existing case law of the ECJ enables the courts with confidence to reach their own decision. The English courts are conscious that (save where no appeal is possible) they have an absolute discretion over whether to refer a question for a preliminary ruling, however difficult they may find the point of law to be. According to the rapporteur, in exercising that discretion, they will have considerable regard to the wishes of the parties and to any adverse consequences that the delay occasioned by the reference could have for the parties or for the administration of justice. No such discretion exists (save where the matter is *acte clair*) before a court against whose decision there is no judicial remedy.

According to the **Belgian** rapporteur, the Council of State does not hesitate to apply the *acte clair* doctrine and to apply Community law directly, which may induce it to reject the demand of parties to refer preliminary questions to the ECJ.[172] Nor will questions be referred if the question is not considered relevant, when Community provisions are not considered applicable in the case at issue, when Belgian provisions oppose themselves to upholding the claim of the party pleading for the referral, or when the act at issue can be annulled on the basis of a violation of the national law, or when national procedural rules dictate otherwise. The Council of State will refer preliminary questions when it considers that a true interpretation difficulty has occurred and when it deems that such referral contributes to the judicial work that has to be realised in co-operation with the ECJ.

The **French** Council of State refers preliminary questions only in the case of serious interpretation problems. In the absence of such a problem or when the existing case law of the ECJ permits it to settle the case, it applies the *acte clair* doctrine. To illustrate, between 1978 and 2001 the Council posed eighteen preliminary questions and applied the *acte clair* doctrine 191 times. Lower administrative courts may ask the Council of State for advice, which may relate to European law. The Council may either give its own answer to the question or deem that the question is of a complex nature and should be referred to the ECJ. Sometimes national courts do not consider it necessary to refer a preliminary question, whereas the case makes clear that there is a serious problem of interpretation.[173] Interestingly, the rapporteur also observes that the preliminary procedure may sometimes be used out of concern that France is the only state to apply particular legislation, such as in the fiscal area, whereas the solution given by the ECJ is imposed upon all Member States.[174] However, in its decisions the administrative court always bases itself on the traditional criteria for reference.[175]

---

[172] See the national report for a number of concrete examples.

[173] E.g., *Chambre syndicale du transport aérien*, 6 January 1997, No. 162553, p. 1.

[174] See the conclusions of 14 December 2001 of commissioner of government Goulard in the case *De Lasteyrie du Saillant*, No. 211341.

[175] In the case mentioned in the previous footnote, the Council of State thus simply referred to 'serious difficulty'.

2.5.2 *Aims*

The relevance of the question what is considered to be the primary aim of the preliminary rulings procedure – i.e., the general interest of uniform application of European law or the individual interest of legal protection – may not seem to be so straightforward. Yet, the answer to this question may certainly have an impact on the scope for possible future amendments of the preliminary procedure or on the direction these amendments would have to take. That is to say, if the main aim of the preliminary procedure is considered to be ensuring individual legal protection, this may lead to an evaluation of, for instance, the proposal to introduce a 'filter' mechanism for referring questions to the ECJ that is different from such an evaluation if the main aim is considered to be ensuring uniform application (see also Chapter 3, section 4.).

A number of rapporteurs observe that the preliminary procedure aims at ensuring both the general interest of uniform interpretation and application of European law and the individual interest of legal protection (**Denmark, Luxemburg, the Netherlands**). The **German** rapporteur in particular points to the protection of individual interests. In **Finland**, the national courts' primary task is to give legal protection to the parties, but the preliminary procedure is mainly seen as serving uniform application of European law. In the last resort, it may also serve legal protection of the individual. No contradiction is considered to exist between these two objectives.

Italian courts as well as the **Portuguese** Supreme Administrative Court, the **Greek** and **French** Councils of State and the **Austrian, Spanish, British** and **Swedish** rapporteurs can be said to perceive the function of the preliminary procedure foremost to be guaranteeing the uniform application of European law. Judge Meij of the CFI also holds this view as may be clear from his observation that, from the perspective of the essential function of Article 234 EC, the primary role of the Community jurisdiction within the framework of the preliminary procedure is to safeguard the unity and the coherence of Community law. The effective protection of individual rights belongs to the competent jurisdiction, in each particular case, be it the national or the Community one (in the case of appeals against Community acts). The **Spanish** rapporteur points to the structural limits of the Article 234 EC procedure, *inter alia*, the inevitably limited capacity of the ECJ. The **Swedish** rapporteur adds to this that the system of preliminary rulings has definitely been established in the abstract interest of uniform application of European law since the courts of last instance are obliged to refer questions, whereas other courts have the possibility to refer questions. In this way, incorrect rulings with effect of precedent can be avoided. The rapporteur thinks that the drafters of the Treaties have not been so naïve as to believe it possible to avoid any wrong decision or ruling by national courts.

The **British** rapporteur observes that the preliminary rulings procedure fulfils both functions, but that ensuring the general interest of uniform application of Community law is most important. Any national court has the power to protect the rights that individuals derive from Community law. Nothing a national court says can, however, ensure the uniform application of Community law: this needs a ruling from the ECJ. The **Belgian** rapporteur notes that the Council of State is well aware of the fact that its use of the preliminary procedure contributes to ensuring the uniformity of Community law, even if preliminary questions are usually induced by claims motivated by the interest of the claimant. The **French** rapporteur points to a case in which the validity of Directive 2002/2/EC was questioned and asked for the reference of preliminary questions on this.[176] With a view to preventing damage to French companies, the Council of State decided to suspend application of the decree that had been adopted to implement this directive and to await the outcome of preliminary questions the British High Court of Justice had already posed on this subject matter.

2.6   What kind of cooperation and consultation – informal or institutionalised?

To what extent does the national court informally consult other persons or organs, both at the national and the European level? To what extent can one speak of an – informal or institutionalised – network of contacts between the highest national courts and the ECJ? (questions 2.2.3 and 2.2.4 of the questionnaire)

Practices vary slightly from one Member State to another regarding the question whether and what forms of informal or institutionalised cooperation or consultation occur between courts on interpretation issues relating to European legislation before submitting preliminary questions. Overall, however, it seems that this kind of cooperation is not highly developed. The national reports show that there is a sufficient basis of support for intensifying this cooperation, even though the form of this cooperation is still a matter for debate (to be elaborated in Chapter 3, section 4.).

In some Member States, informal consultation or networks, both at the national and the European levels, are virtually non-existent (**Denmark, Italy, Germany, France, the UK, Belgium**). The **Finnish** Supreme Administrative Court may contact other national courts in order to find out whether similar cases are pending, but there is no established system of exchange of information

---

[176] Council of State, 29 October 2003, *Société Techna S.A. et autres*, No. 260768.

on European law matters. The ECJ has also been consulted with a view to obtaining information on the cases pending before it. In **Portugal**, exchange of views takes place with university professors or colleagues having previous experience with a particular matter. It is also observed that direct contacts between national jurisdictions and the ECJ is now more intense than before, in particular as a result of electronic means which allow national judges not only to be informed about final ECJ judgments but also, step by step almost, to follow the developments in interesting pending cases. In **Spain** as well, informal consultation of other judges occurs and sometimes the Commission is contacted in the framework of state aid or competition law cases. A network of contacts is certainly considered beneficial, but cannot replace the Article 234 procedure. In **Austria**, informal contacts are said to occur now and then. In **Sweden**, no formal consultation outside the court takes place before posing questions. In **the Netherlands**, judges from different courts come together to discuss cases afterwards (a kind of consultation of peers). The **Greek** rapporteur also observes that there are no formal ways of consulting the ECJ, but that in some rare instances members of the Council of State contact persons in the Court with a view to obtaining information that is not available on the Internet. The **Belgian** rapporteur states that such contacts limit themselves to inquiring whether a European provision has already been the subject of a preliminary ruling or whether such question is pending before the ECJ, in order to avoid an unnecessary reference.

The **British** rapporteur observes to be unaware of whether such informal contacts take place and that if they do, they must be very rare. It would generally be seen by English judges as contrary to the principle that judicial decision-making should be open and transparent and not be influenced by informal contacts of which the litigants are unaware and on which they cannot comment. Yet, he also observes that the current UK judge in the ECJ was, until recently, a judge of the English Court of Appeal and that judges from other Member States have been frequent visitors to England and have good contacts with the academic and judicial communities in London. There is also an active programme of judicial visits from England to the ECJ, including at the most senior levels.

3.   ATTACHING CONSEQUENCES TO INTERPRETATION ERRORS

Despite the efforts to prevent problems of interpretation and to solve them when they do arise, it must be acknowledged at the same time that errors of interpretation cannot be excluded. This applies both in the field of legislation and in the field of the administration of justice. For example, it may emerge in a case before the national court that, wrongly, no preliminary questions were posed or that an interpretation followed by the national legislature in the course of the implementation was incorrect. The question which then arises, and to be addressed in this section, is what consequences should be attached to the observation of such errors. Does it give rise to the establishment of the liability of the national court and/or legislature or to starting an infringement action against the Member State, also in the case of a national court making an interpretation error? Although there is no hierarchical relationship between the ECJ and the national courts, it is clear that the precedence of European law over national law must be ensured. One general question that can be posed in this regard is what contribution a (better) *ex post* evaluation of European and national implementing legislation can make to combating problems of interpretation and as such also to improving the quality of legislation?

3.1   *Ex post* examination of legislation

How to ensure the correction of shortcomings in transposition legislation which the Council of State or other national courts may have noted? Is this picked up by the national legislature and are consequences attached? (question 3.1.1 questionnaire)

It appears that in some Member States the national legislature is inclined to attach consequences to national court findings of shortcomings in implementation. The **Finnish** rapporteur thus observes that correction of shortcomings in transposition legislation is partly a matter of information, partly a matter of political will. The Finnish political system is relatively well informed and aware of such shortcomings as there is a special coordination system uniting all ministries for the preparation of Finland's positions in infringement proceedings and ECJ cases. The Ministry of Foreign Affairs also biannually prepares a report concerning all ECJ cases and Commission proceedings involving Finland, which are sent to parliament. Of course, if the supreme courts find that a particular European act has not been transposed or has not been transposed correctly, the relevant ministry takes note of the decision and this may then lead to a legislative reaction. After either the national supreme courts or the ECJ has established the shortcoming, the government is obliged to take the necessary legislative steps. An example of this is provided by the reform of the car tax regime after the Supreme Administrative Court found the regime to be incompatible with the EC Treaty,[177] following the preliminary ruling of the ECJ in the *Tulliasiamies and Antti Siilin* case.[178]

---

[177] KHO 2002:85.
[178] Ibid. n. 71.

Likewise, the **German** federal government takes note of the judgments of the Federal Administrative Court, and if this Court has noted shortcomings in the transposition of European law, the federal government will take the appropriate action that may include legislative proposals. This is facilitated by the appointment of a representative of the federal interest at the Federal Administrative Court. In **the Netherlands** too, judgments by national courts on the unlawfulness of national legislation often lead to a reaction of the legislature. Yet, since discussions on incomplete or incorrect transposition of national rules with European rules occur along different tracks – through national court proceedings and European infringement proceedings –, the court proceeding is frequently caught up with an amendment procedure of the legislation. According to the **Austrian** rapporteur, it may be assumed that the competent government authorities will draw the conclusions necessary from the decisions of the Administrative Court and the shortcomings in implementation, which are indicated therein. Up to now, these shortcomings have not been published in the Court's annual reports. When the **French** Council of State has noted a shortcoming in transposition, it makes sure that the administrative authorities and the legislature conform to European law. Case law shows numerous examples of this requirement, in particular as regards directives.[179] The **British** rapporteur notes that in cases where judges have had to disapply provisions of implementing legislation in order to give effect to Community law,[180] revised legislation will normally follow (once appeal rights have been exhausted) as a matter of course. Where judicial criticism is directed more to the complexity or obscurity of implementing legislation than to its illegality, a reaction from government cannot be guaranteed. However, the Law Commission – a body of legal experts, chaired by a High Court judge and responsible for keeping the law under review and recommending changes were necessary – may have a useful role to play.

In **Belgium**, the competent ministries will sollicit the informal advice of the European Commission on bills proposed for the transposition of directives, before their submission to the government, but this consultation does not take place in a systematic way. Furthermore, the appointment of a European coordinator in each ministry has led to a certain level of specialisation within the administration, which also contributes to the prevention of transposition difficulties. The legislative department of the Council of State plays an important role as well, since draft bills are submitted to it for advice, thus including virtually all texts aimed at the transposition of directives. The Council's (non-

---

[179] See, e.g., the judgment of 29 June 2001, *Vassilikiotis*, No. 213229, p. 303, and CE 6/4 SSR, 27 July 2001, *Titran*, No. 222509.
[180] E.g., Case *Hodgson v. CCE*, [1997] EuLR 117.

binding) advice includes the assessment of their comformity with European law. Political authorities will respond to possible objections that have been raised in this regard, either by modifying their proposals or by motivating why they take a different view than the Council of State. The Belgian rapporteur states that this system seems sufficient and that there is considered to be no need to create an additional level for checking this conformity.

The **Greek** rapporteur observes that there is no mechanism in force, which allows systematic information of the government on the judgments and advice the Council of State issues and which signal a defect in respect of European law. The annual report on the Council of State's activities could fill this gap. Only in cases in which the government (a ministry) is directly involved – in legal proceedings or because a regulatory decree has been submitted for advice – the judgment or advice of the Council of State will be notified. Yet, a commission of legal experts, attached to the Secretariat-General of the government, and the scientific service of the House of Representatives examine proposals for legislation and also their compatibility with European law. Furthermore, by Law 3133/2003 a central Commission for codification has been established, which is to review the existing, expanded body of legislation. Within this framework, national rules that are not compatible with European law can be drawn to the attention of the government as well. Nonetheless, the rapporteur deems that the creation of a central organ charged with the coordination and check of the transposition and application of European legislation, would facilitate and accelerate harmonisation efforts.

Since the **Portuguese** Supreme Administrative Court does not have a legislation advisory function, it can only in a concrete case state that the transposition legislation falls short of the European law requirements and attach consequences to this.[181] Such court decisions are considered to have no effect whatsoever on the national legislature, which may even persist in not remedying the shortcomings established in the transposition process without any sanction. In **Spain**, the legislature will remedy shortcomings in national transposition legislation only after an infringement procedure or a preliminary ruling has brought these to light. Yet, in the area of penal law, Article 4 of the Penal Code enables the judge to communicate to the government alleged omissions in the law, possibly in the light of European law.

What notice is taken in the administration of justice of shortcomings in national transposition legislation, which have been established by the European Com-

---

[181] See, e.g., the judgment of the Supreme Administrative Court of 7 January 2003, No. 34368.

mission or otherwise? Can an authority or agency be designated which periodically reports on this, so that shortcomings can be remedied? (question 3.1.2 questionnaire)

In addition to what was observed above as regards **Finland**, it can be noted that the Finnish Supreme Administrative Court studies the correctness of national implementation *ex officio*, when it applies the relevant national implementation legislation for the first time. If it is satisfied with the implementation, the issue is not raised in later cases, unless the parties challenge the implementation or the Court has become aware of possible shortcomings. The rapporteur excludes the possibility that the Supreme Administrative Court would be unaware of claims concerning possible shortcomings in national implementation legislation. The situation of lower administrative courts is probably worse in this respect. In the aforementioned *Tulliasiamies and Antti Siilin* case, the Supreme Administrative Court declared the national legislation inapplicable in so far as it was incompatible with the EC Treaty. Yet, there may also be cases in which the Court takes note of incomplete or incorrect implementation, but where this does not influence the outcome of the case.[182]

The **Dutch** rapporteur is of the opinion that, although a pattern may be discernable after a number of proceedings, the judge is not in a position to report this to the legislature in a general way. There is no institutionalised framework for *ex post* evaluation of legislation. The ministries and legal doctrine fulfil this function. The **Swedish** rapporteur made a similar observation, stating that it should not be the task of national courts to adjust or correct erroneous implementation of European law; they should ensure that individuals are able to enjoy the rights they have on the basis of European law. The speed with which the legislature reacts to such cases differs, although normally the error will be corrected. He further considers that the fact that the Commission criticises national implementation does not mean that the implementation is wrongful and should not as such influence the national courts.

The **Portuguese** rapporteur observes that in the case the Commission started infringement proceedings for shortcomings in implementation, the national court will analyse the question and where necessary draw the consequences required. He also advocates better information supply about the stage infringe-

---

[182] Cf., case KHO 2003:38, in which the Supreme Administrative Court established that Art. 12(1)(d) of Directive 92/43/EEC had been incorrectly implemented, in so far as the applicable national legislation protected only clearly perceptible resting places and breeding sites of flying squirrels. In that case, however, the existence of such resting places and breeding sites in the wood concerned was undisputed and, as a result, this shortcoming did not have material effects on the decision.

ment proceedings are in, because national courts often lack this information.[183] The **Greek** Council of State may inquire about this at the special legal service of the Ministry of Foreign Affairs. In **Spain**, there is no official channel for communicating information on infringement proceedings engaged against the Spanish State. Yet, Article 226 EC judgments facilitate the work of national courts, as preliminary reference with a view to finding out whether national legislation is in conformity with European law in that case is no longer required. The **French** rapporteur notes that the annual report that is now being drawn up by the EU delegation of the National Assembly on the non-transposition and incomplete transposition of directives takes the implementation record drawn up by the Commission as its main basis. It also appears that the threat of the Commission initiating an infringement procedure puts pressure on both the legislature and the courts to act in conformity with EC law. The **Belgian** rapporteur notes that, in Belgium, no institutionalised system exists for taking account of shortcomings in implementation that have been established by the European Commission or by any other institution. However, there are other information mechanisms which inform the national jurisdictions and the legislative department of the Council of State on the existence of infringement proceedings.[184]

The **Austrian** rapporteur also observes that it may be a problem as to how the court gets to know the observations of the Commission. If there are such observations, the court may take a decision only in compliance with the *CILFIT* criteria. Furthermore, he expresses serious doubts about the possibility and functionality of an institutionalised check or a periodical report on shortcomings in implementation, pointing in particular to the fact that individual cases often reveal questions of detail which may not result from a general monitoring of shortcomings.[185] It is considered illusory to think that general monitoring will lead to the identification of all possible shortcomings, yet it might be helpful in revealing and avoiding structural shortcomings. A comprehensive survey of individual cases to determine certain structural weaknesses might also be a good idea. With a view to this, existing periodical reviews of the decisions of the Administrative Court could be extended, for instance by establishing a kind of agency that analyses the court's decisions.

In **Italy**, the Minister responsible for the coordination of European policies is responsible not only for transmitting the normative EU acts to parliament, but

---

[183] See also the suggestion made in Chapter 3, section 3.

[184] See the Belgian report for a more detailed discussion.

[185] Illustrations of this are the decisions of 20 February 2003, 2001/07/0171 concerning environmental impact assessment and of 20 November 2002, 2001/17/0180 concerning credit institutions.

also for verifying the conformity of the internal legal order with European law and for transmitting in due time the outcome of these verifications to parliament, while suggesting or putting forward measures or initiatives to be developed (see also section 1.3). As a result, notification by the Council of State or other national courts of particular shortcomings in the implementation or application of a European norm, possibly identified by the Commission or another institution, obliges the Minister to act and engages its political responsibility.

The **British** rapporteur states that unlawful implementation identified by the European Commission, if not corrected, may generally be expected to lead to infringement proceedings under Article 226 EC. Unlawful implementation identified by national courts will normally result in revised legislation. The Law Commission can recommend changes to the law, including the law implementing Community obligations. This seems to be a broadly satisfactory framework.

As regards **Germany**, see the observations made above in section 2.4.

> *What contribution can* ex post *examination of both European and national implementation legislation make to improved implementation and application of European legislation? Is the examination that takes place at present satisfactory both at the European and the national levels?* (question 3.1.3 questionnaire)

It follows from a number of national reports that the check performed by judges, both at the national and the European levels is considered quite satisfactory. More in general, the **Finnish** rapporteur considers that *ex post* examination improves the legislative standards applied in implementation and provides useful information for courts and others having to apply European law. He expresses the fear that, at the European level, examination is too much focused on the legislative failures of the Member States and not enough on the reasons for these shortcomings and whether they can be reduced by improving the quality of European legislation and the decision-making processes leading to adoption thereof. The **Swedish** rapporteur observes that we all, including the legislature, learn by our mistakes and that therefore *ex post* examination of implementation measures is of value for the future, both at the national and the European levels. The **German** rapporteur considers that *ex post* checking is an effective instrument for improvement. The check judges perform at both the national level and the European level is in fact a check which occurs accidentally, but which is perfectly capable of drawing the legislature's attention to the truly important issues. The **Luxemburg** rapporteur also thinks that the present system of judicial and administrative checking is satisfactory as it allows, among other things, checking the conformity of national transposition legislation with European law, possibly after having referred preliminary questions. Likewise, the **Italian** rapporteur is of the opinion that the ECJ actually created a fantastic system of *ex post* checking of the transposition and application of European law, by establishing the possibility of state liability in the case of legislative, executive or judicial failure in respect of European law obligations. *Ex post* checking can thus be exercised by those directly concerned with the application of European law.

However, there also seems room for improvement of *ex post* examination of legislation. The **Dutch** rapporteur is of the opinion that the structuring and organisation of the input of national courts, resulting from their experience with the application of European and national legislation, may have an added value. The **Austrian** rapporteur considers that examination by the courts takes place at a time when specific problems in individual cases have already arisen. Intensified *ex post* examination may contribute to preventing these problems in the first place. The **Portuguese** rapporteur thinks that the Commission already conducts *ex post* examinations of European legislation and national implementation legislation. Yet, national courts' findings that transposition legislation has shortcomings should also be communicated to the Commission and to the ECJ, and an accelerated injunction mechanism should be put into place with a view to forcing Member States to adapt to the national legislation if the finding of the national court is considered well founded.

The **Greek** rapporteur deems that there should be qualified institutions for examining systematically the problems that arise in respect of the application of European law and between European law and national law, taking both a European and a national perspective. More reflection should take place on how checking the application of European law can be generalised. The **French** rapporteur thinks that a closer scrutiny of Community legislation is compatible with the principle of subsidiarity. Yet, as regards national transposition legislation he suggests that a true policy of evaluating the quality of transposition be developed, uniting the Community institutions, governments and parliaments. The delegation of the National Assembly dealing with EU affairs asked, without success, to put this issue on the agenda of the Conference of organs dealing with European affairs, held in Rome on October 2003. The **Belgian** rapporteur suggests that the Belgian governments should keep better record of the transposition difficulties as these result from the advice of the legislative section of the Council of State and of the judicial and administrative jurisdictions. Such record should be coupled with adequate publicity and parliamentary control mechanisms, allowing for the necessary legislative initiatives.

3.2 National repair mechanism: the liability of national legislatures and courts

What are the possibilities of obtaining compensation in the case of erroneous interpretation of European law, both by the court and by the legislature? (question 3.2.2 of the questionnaire)

In their report, Judges Puissochet and Timmermans observe first of all that it may be interesting to have an overview of the cases in which the *Brasserie* state liability case law of the Court has been applied in the Member States. Next, they note the fact that the national rapporteurs consider the *Köbler* case law to be far more innovating than the *Brasserie* case law, in particular because, in most legal systems, the principle of state liability has one exception: that of the authority of *res judicata*. Furthermore, they note that legal scholars argue that the Court has engaged itself in a quasi-hierarchical control of national supreme courts, which is alien to the preliminary rulings system and to the *dialogue des juges*. In their view, however, the critical remarks which the *Köbler* judgment has inspired from both these perspectives are not considered justified, *inter alia*, because liability proceedings have to be distinguished from the previous proceedings and because the new proceedings cannot call into question the *res judicata* and can only allow for financial compensation. They state further that the *Köbler* case law seems disturbing particularly because of the effects it may have in the Member States on the relations between the supreme courts and the lower courts; the lower court may have to rule on the state's liability as a result of a higher court having committed a manifest error in applying Community law. It is considered that these difficulties of a psychological and institutional nature are indeed real and will have to be solved by adapting national procedural law. A new *Köbler*-type of case is now pending.[186]

From the national reports one may conclude that, overall, the possibility of obtaining compensation for erroneous interpretation of European law by national courts and the legislature is provided for by national law or recognised on the basis of the *Francovich* and *Köbler* judgments of the ECJ,[187] which is not to say that concrete cases have come up. Furthermore, the conditions under which compensation can be claimed may differ.

In **Portugal**, individuals can claim damages from the government if they became the victims of a lack of transposition, incorrect transposition or erro-

---

[186] Case C-173/03 *Traghetti del Mediterraneo,* still pending.
[187] Cases C-6/90 and C-9/90 *Francovich and Bonifaci v. Italy,* ECR [1991] I-5357 and Case C-224/01 *Köbler,* ECR [2003] I-10239.

neous interpretation by the national court, by starting a procedure for wrongful act under the usual conditions.

Article 121 of the **Spanish** Constitution explicitly confirms the possibility of compensation in the case of a judicial error, which may be claimed whenever the judicial error has not been repaired upon appeal and has caused effective damages that can be quantified and individualised. The claim for compensation must be preceded by a decision of the Supreme Court, recognising the existence of an error.[188]

The **Danish** Supreme Court is not aware of any such case having occurred as yet, but if it does occur, it would have to be judged on the basis of the normal conditions for obtaining compensation in the case of errors made by a public authority. The basic condition is that a public authority acted negligently, so erroneous interpretation in itself will not be sufficient. Liability in the case of erroneous interpretation of European law by parliament is considered unthinkable.

In **Greece**, a claimant can avail himself of the ordinary – appeal or cassation – procedures if a wrong interpretation of European law has been given by an administrative court. If it concerns the Council of State, the Court of Auditors or the administrative court ruling in last instance, then a special procedure is provided before a court which consists of the President of the Council of State, a Councillor of State, a judge of the Court of Cassation, a Councillor of the Court of Auditors, two university professors and two lawyers. Yet, it is very difficult to obtain compensation since intentional error has to be proven on the part of the judge, a condition that is rarely fulfilled in practice. In view of this, the rapporteur thinks it necessary to create a special procedure, in order to enable claimants to obtain compensation in the case of irrevocable judgments which are based on erroneous interpretation of European law.

In **Luxemburg**, state liability and the right to compensation for wrongful application of a legal rule can be based on the Law on civil liability of public authorities. Yet, the Law on civil liability of the state contains a reservation as regards the authority of judgments.

In **France**, liability of national courts can be established on the basis of Article 11 of the Law of 5 July 1972, which requires the establishment of a serious error. In fact, the refusal to put final judgments to the test again and the require-

---

[188] In two cases state liability for infringement of European law was established, yet not attributable to the judiciary: judgment of the *Audience Nationale* of 7 May 2002 (non-transposition of Directive 94/47) and judgment of the Supreme Court of 12 June 2003 (national laws contrary to Arts. 28 and 49 EC and Directive 83/189/EEC). In both cases, the courts apparently deemed the one-year time limit for starting the liability procedure to be in accordance with the European principle of effectiveness.

ment of serious error make that, up to now, it has never been able to conclude to liability of the state for a bad interpretation of – national or European – law.[189]

Dutch liability law is stricter than the judgment in the *Francovich* case: when the national court annuls an administrative decision, the decision's unlawfulness and the administration's ensuing liability can be assumed either by a civil or an administrative court. The same goes for Dutch legislation that is held to be unlawful. Stricter conditions apply, however, in the case of liability on the basis of unlawful case law. This possibility is actually limited to situations in which the national court infringes on fundamental rights when dealing with a case, in particular Articles 5 and 6 of the ECHR. As such, this concerns the court's procedures, not the substance of the judgment. So, the *Köbler* decision may have more far-reaching consequences for Dutch legal practice.

In **Finland**, liability of the legislature for erroneous interpretation of European law is covered by the *Francovich* judgment, but so far no concrete cases have been tried. Actions against the State on this ground in the late 1990s were all dropped even before the court of first instance gave its ruling. Erroneous interpretation of European law by national courts is covered by Chapter 3 of the Torts Act, which contains the obligation to pay damages because of erroneous exercise of public authority. This Chapter excludes compensation if the person concerned did not appeal against the judicial decision and the decision was not amended or repealed because of the appeal. Furthermore, if a person appealed against an administrative decision on the ground of erroneous interpretation of European law and lost his or her case, but still the interpretation of European law by the administrative courts turns out to be erroneous (e.g., because of a new ruling by the ECJ), then their judgments can be reversed. In most cases, the economic damage has already been corrected when the erroneous administrative or fiscal decision is corrected.

In the **UK**, the possibility of obtaining compensation in the event of an erroneous interpretation of Community law by the legislature is illustrated by the Joined cases C-46/93 and C-48/93.[190] After the ECJ's judgment in this case, the Divisional Court, followed by the Court of Appeal and House of Lords, found that the error of law in the Merchant Shipping Act 1988, being both grave and manifest, was sufficiently serious to sound in damages. Damages were subsequently recovered. The principle that government may be liable for manifest errors of Community law committed by national supreme courts, as the ECJ

---

[189] See the French report for a more detailed discussion of this and also of possible liability of the administration and the legislature.

[190] Joined cases C-46/93 and C-48/93 *Brasserie du Pêcheur SA v Bundesrepublik Deutschland and The Queen v Secretary of State for Transport, ex parte: Factortame Ltd and others,* ECR [1996] I-1029.

established in the *Köbler* case, has led to one such claim for damages being brought already in the UK, founded upon the refusal of the House of Lords to grant permission to appeal against an order of the Court of Appeal. Two features of the English judicial system are likely to render it difficult for *Köbler*-type cases to be resolved in England: its doctrine of *stare decisis* (meaning that lower courts are accustomed to treating the decisions of higher courts as strictly binding upon them) and its unitary nature (civil and administrative courts all forming part of the same judicial hierarchy). Indeed, it has been questioned whether a lower court which is called upon to decide whether a higher court committed an excusable error of Community law would, in the context of the English legal system, have the requisite independence to satisfy, e.g., Article 6 ECHR. Nevertheless the rapporteur does not doubt that the English courts will loyally apply the principles of the case law in this area, even if the resolution of *Köbler*-type cases requires questions to be referred to the ECJ so as to avoid or minimise the problems identified.

The **Belgian** rapporteur notes that, ever since the Court of Cassation rendered the *La Flandria* judgment on 5 November 1920,[191] it has developed case law as a result of which public authorities can be held liable under civil law. Consequently, every misuse of power, that is, the violation of a higher rule of law, constitutes a wrongful act. In a judgment of 19 December 1991, the Court of Cassation also explicitly established this principle as regards the liability for errors committed within the exercise of the judicial function.[192] Still, the conditions under which it has deemed such actions for liability admissible pose difficulties.[193] Therefore, and also with a view to ensuring conformity of Belgian law with Community law requirements as they follow from the *Köbler* judgment, the rapporteur argues that the legislation should be adapted. As regards the liability of the legislature for violations of Community law, the Court of Cassation has not yet rendered any judgment of principle on this.

Some national reports give the impression that entitlement to compensation for wrongful implementation and interpretation of European law in their Member States relies foremost on ECJ's case law on state liability (**Sweden, Austria, Germany, Italy**). The **Austrian** rapporteur thus notes that the discussion on liability for damages has become more intense after the *Köbler* judgment and the later decisions of the Constitutional Court, in which it held that in the case of a European law failure of the legislature the Constitutional Court is competent to decide on state liability[194] and that this competence also applies

---

[191] *Pasicrisie (Pas.)*, 1920, I, p. 239.
[192] *J.T.*, 1992, pp. 142-152.
[193] See the Belgian report for a detailed discussion of this.
[194] Decision of 7 October 2003, A 11/01.

in cases where the claim is based on a decision by the Supreme Court, the Administrative Court or the Constitutional Court.[195] Under **German** law, damages can only be obtained in the case of unlawful infringement of the law, which cannot be concluded upon in the case it is a national court that made an interpretation error. Yet, the German rapporteur considers the strict conditions under which the ECJ has created this possibility in the *Köbler* case acceptable. The **Italian** rapporteur is of the same opinion, considering that, on the one hand, the Court confirmed the responsibility of the state for acts of the legislature and the decisions of the highest national jurisdictions, while on the other, leaving the establishment of the existence of a 'manifest violation' of European law to the judgment of the national court. In doing so, the ECJ has remained respectful of the national legal orders, demonstrating that the aim of its case law is not to sanction or to repair, but only to establish an instrument that contributes to the uniform application of European law.

3.3   Revision possibility in the case of liability of the national court

Should there be a specific revision possibility, apart from the existing applicability of Article 234 EC, or a higher provision with the ECJ to adjudicate on such issues? (question 3.2.3 of the questionnaire)

There appears to be no basis of support for the introduction of a revision possibility at the level of the ECJ in the case of liability of a national court for erroneous interpretation of European law, albeit that different arguments for the rejection of this idea are put forward.

The **German**, **Danish**, **Dutch**, **Austrian** and **Swedish** rapporteurs do not think it necessary to introduce a specific or higher provision with the Court of Justice to adjudicate on such cases; national courts are capable of handling these or at least the required revision possibilities should be created pursuant to the *Köbler* judgment. The **Italian** rapporteur does not think it necessary not only because it would prejudice the authority of national courts, but also because it would mean introducing an additional and inappropriate remedy at the European level in the framework of a national procedure. The **Dutch** rapporteur adds that it would also undermine the preliminary procedure. In the opinion of the **Finnish** rapporteur, every legal system has to cope with the fact that the courts may issue erroneous judgments and that some of them may remain final. Every reform that would increase the workload of the ECJ should be opposed. The **Greek** rapporteur also points to the latter risk. It is thought preferable to

---

[195] Decision of 10 October 2003, A 36/00.

issue a directive that obliges the Member States to adopt the necessary rules with a view to the matter at issue, while respecting their procedural autonomy. The **Portuguese** rapporteur considers it preferable to reinforce the mechanism of the infringement procedure with a view to this and to promote the use of liability actions.

The **British** rapporteur observes that, in the UK, there is judicial reluctance to award damages in respect of acts of the government or the legislature. If such a problem does exist in other Member States, he doubts whether the solution lies in the invention of a new procedure whereby the ECJ or the CFI would have original jurisdiction in an action for damages at the suit of individuals against a Member State. He considers that such a procedure would be cumbersome and could engender significant ill-will. A more pragmatic solution is considered to be that the ECJ, in deciding infringement actions, would state of its own initiative, in deserving cases, that the infringement in question would appear at least at first sight to meet the requirements for liability. The Court took this course in Case C-265/95, *Commission v. France*, in which it held (despite the fact that damages were not directly in issue) that the national government in question had 'manifestly and persistently abstained from adopting appropriate and adequate measures to put an end to the acts of vandalism which jeopardise the free movement on its territory of certain agricultural products originating in other Member States and to prevent the recurrence of such acts'.[196] By the use of such language, the ECJ facilitated a subsequent damages action in the national court, if one were to be brought. Furthermore, if such a damages action were rejected by the supreme court, the conditions for *Köbler* liability in respect of that rejection would then be easier for the claimant to satisfy.

Judges Puissochet and Timmermans observe that attributing such a new competence to the Community courts would clash with the present rules on the division of the jurisdictional competences between the EU and the Member States. Apart from the jurisdictional burden it would impose, it would also require a modification of the Treaty.

However, the **Luxemburg** rapporteur sees advantages, from the viewpoint of uniform application of criteria and solutions. The **Belgian** rapporteur also argues that, for reasons of efficacy, certainty, and coherence, the ECJ should not only be able to establish the fault of a jurisdiction in the framework of infringement proceedings, but also have a new competence conferred on it allowing it to examine whether national supreme jurisdictions have respected Community law.

---

[196] Case C-265/95 *Commission v. France,* ECR [1997] I-6959.

3.4   Possible European repair mechanisms

Should the European Commission in the case of interpretation errors by the national courts make use of the possibility of launching an Article 226 EC infringement procedure against a Member State for infringement of European law? (question 3.2.1 of the questionnaire)

The general impression raised by the national reports is that it cannot be excluded that the Commission will start Article 226 EC proceedings in the case of interpretation errors by national courts, but that it should do so only in very serious cases and that anyway it will be of limited, even symbolic importance only. Some rapporteurs also advise against this use. Furthermore, attention is drawn to the risk of damaging the cooperation relationship between the national courts and the ECJ, which is the real cornerstone of the efficacy of European law, and of possibly causing a constitutional crisis in the Union (**Finland, France**). Yet, it should be noted that, meanwhile, the ECJ has rendered judgment in the *Commission v. Italy* case,[197] which the Commission initiated, *inter alia*, because of the way in which particular Italian courts applied and interpreted Law 428/1990. The Court held that this Law is constructed and applied by the administrative authorities and a substantial proportion of the courts, including the *Corte suprema di cassazione*, in such a way that the exercise of the right to repayment of charges levied in breach of Community rules is made excessively difficult for the taxpayer. Consequently, Italy has failed to fulfil its obligations under the EC Treaty. In February 2004, the Commission decided to start an infringement procedure against the Netherlands for wrongful interpretation of Regulation 1408/71 by the Dutch *Hoge Raad*.[198]

Judges Puissochet and Timmermans observe that in fact the question at issue in the *Commission v. Italy* case had already been decided in the case law, since it was established case law that an infringement of Community law by a Member State can be established irrespective of what state agency is responsible for this infringement. This even goes for constitutionally independent institutions.[199] It was thus difficult not to include the jurisdictional institutions in this case law, the more so since the Court had just recognised in the *Köbler* case the possibility of holding the state liable for a manifest error of Community law committed by a supreme jurisdiction. Unlike in the *Köbler* case, the Court did not have to deal with the issue of state liability in the case of a judicial error, but

---

[197] Case C-129/00 *Commission v. Italy,* judgment of 9 December 2003, not yet reported. See also the Spanish report on this case.
[198] See press release IP/04/178, 9 February 2004.
[199] See Case 77/69 *Commission v. Belgium,* ECR [1970] 237.

it had only to examine whether an objective situation of infringement of Community law existed at the date fixed in the Commission's reasoned opinion and sent to the defending state.

They emphasise further that, in the judgment in the *Commission v. Italy* case, the Court concentrated in particular on two questions, which can be said to provide a basis for the analysis of other cases as well. Firstly, the Court examined who was to be held responsible for the infringement; did the infringement result solely from the jurisdictional decisions or was it primarily caused by the legislature who had adopted a law that allowed infringements of Community law? The Court adopted a middle road in this respect, by stating, on the one hand, that the dominant interpretation of the *Corte suprema di cassazione* was not in line with the case law of the ECJ and, on the other, that the Italian legislature should have tackled this situation by modifying the Italian law allowing this interpretation. Even though the Court thus seemed to favour an approach on the basis of a global analysis of the scope that provisions have in the national legal order, in their view it cannot be excluded that, in a future case, the Court may establish a pure 'judicial infringement', when a wrongful application of Community law is to be attributed exclusively to the jurisdiction, for instance, if it fails to recognise the primacy of Community law.

Secondly, the Court had to examine what judicial decisions can constitute an infringement of Community law. In this regard, it is made clear in paragraph 32 of the judgment, that 'isolated or numerically insignificant judicial decisions in the context of case law taking a different direction, or still more a construction disowned by the national supreme court, cannot be taken into account. That is not true of a widely-held judicial construction which has not been disowned by the supreme court, but rather confirmed by it'. The principle is thus admitted that the Commission can start infringement proceedings aimed directly at judicial decisions that have a significant scope in the Member State and which reflect the way in which Community law is applied in that Member State. As such, Judges Puissochet and Timmermans acknowledge that this may have a considerable institutional impact and may even raise constitutional problems in the Member States, but they also argue that the Commission can be expected to make reasonable use of this possibility and that infringement proceedings based on judicial errors will not be numerous and will be limited to those cases involving clearly established errors or refusals to apply Community law.

The **British** rapporteur observes that he has no difficulty with the Court's ruling in the *Commission v. Italy* case, though he also considers that the remedy is a constitutionally delicate one and will probably not be frequently used. He is further of the opinion that there are risks of confusing the separate responsibilities of the executive (the Commission), the legislatures (of the Community and at the national levels) and the judiciaries of the national courts. Reference to a higher court is the usual mechanism for correcting errors of law by a lower court. However, in the UK, it is left to the parties to make the decision about an appeal and there is no procedure for cases to be 'called in' by a higher court. It is then left to the legislature to pass amending legislation if it does not agree with the judgments of the courts.

The **Swedish** rapporteur observes that there is nothing that formally prevents the Commission from starting an infringement procedure. Whether that should be done, must depend on the gravity of the infringement and it should be up to the Commission to decide if and how it should be done. In this regard a structural or very fundamental infringement of European law (**the Netherlands**) and manifest interpretation errors (**Greece**) are mentioned. The **Austrian** rapporteur does not deem it appropriate for the Association to give any recommendation on this issue, as the decision whether or not to start such proceedings is always up to the Commission. The **Finnish** rapporteur strongly advises against this use, considering that given the number of cases in which European law is applied in the Member States, there are probably hundreds or thousands of interpretation errors yearly. So, a Commission reaction would be realistic only in cases in which one can speak of a very erroneous interpretation by a *mala fide* supreme jurisdiction. The **Italian** rapporteur considers that it concerns an instrument of primarily emblematic value, too frequent use of which would reduce its impact.

The **Portuguese** rapporteur also considers it a remedy in the last resort, after having first tried to solve the issue of erroneous interpretation by the national court by means of internal procedures and to be used only when national courts persist in a wrongful interpretation. The **German** rapporteur states that the possibility of having a wrong judgment, originating in an interpretation error, cannot be avoided in any legal system. When all appeal possibilities have been tried, the *Rechtsstaat* demands that the case be ended. Initiating an infringement procedure at that point is considered to go against the principle of respecting the authority of the final judgment (in a similar sense **France**). Furthermore, the German State would be in a difficult position in executing such an infringement judgment, as it would oppose it to the national jurisdiction. It is also considered difficult to understand why a claimant who suffered a violation of his or her European law rights would necessitate a higher level of legal protection than a claimant that suffered a violation of a right protected by national law.

Chapter 3
CONCLUSIONS AND SOLUTIONS

1.   THE MAIN CONCLUSIONS

In this final Part, the lines of the preceding sections will first be drawn together, presenting the main conclusions regarding the various quality or interpretation issues that European legislation poses for the national courts and legislatures which were briefly identified in Chapter 1, section 1.2.

It became clear that the problems that arise in the national contexts as regards the implementation and application of European legislation are attributable to the poor quality of European legislation only to a limited extent, relating to rather technical aspects such as the definition and use of ambiguous, complex and vague concepts, problems of translation, consistency, etc. For instance, the Habitat Directive has thus been criticised for its vagueness and complicated system of designating potential areas for protection. More in particular, the conclusion appears justified that such quality problems of European legislation are only part of a bigger problem, which is the general difficulty encountered in the Member States to determine the right meaning and scope of European legislation, i.e., the appropriate interpretation thereof, which may be caused by quite a number of other factors. These originate both in the European and in the national legal systems and in the fact that these systems are still not very well geared to one another.

Other aspects the national rapporteurs therefore considered problematic at the European level were the important judge-made nature of European law, the perceived lack of balance or inconsistency between ECJ case law and the general nature of the legislation, and the lack of *travaux préparatoires*. Problems of alignment have become obvious for instance in the case of the same terminology being used in European and national legislations, but having a different meaning in the national legislation. The transposition of the Sixth VAT Directive also shows that problems arose in particular in those Member States which chose to maintain the system, structure and terminology of the national law on this type of taxation. Rather surprising in view of the recent proposals of the European Convention on reforming and introducing a hierarchy of the European legal instruments, is the fact that the lack of an explicit hierarchy of sources is not perceived as very problematic and does not appear to have posed any particular problems for national courts and legislatures. This does not alter the fact that the introduction of such a hierarchy may be of importance from other perspectives, such as the protection against the undermining of the division of competences as a result of the use of tertiary, soft EU law.

At the national level, state-specific factors which add to the problems of implementing and interpreting European legislation – and can thus not be remedied at the European level – concern the different levels of internal decision-making in federal systems (such as the Spanish, German, Austrian and Belgium systems) and the accession of Member States after European legislation had been adopted (Finland). The transposition of the Bird and Habitat Directives provides a clear illustration of this, as in federal systems this was seriously delayed and/or complicated. Furthermore, for a state that fairly recently became a Member State, like Finland, it meant that not only the Finnish legislation had to be adapted to the European directives, but European legislation had to be adapted to incorporate the circumstances of Finnish nature as well.

On the basis of the national reports, it is difficult to establish a general correlation between the chosen method of transposition and the magnitude and nature of the interpretation and application problems the national courts will later be confronted with. However, the case study on the Sixth VAT Directive shows that in certain instances such a correlation can actually be established. More generally, it appears that national practices may vary quite a bit as to the choice of transposition method. This choice depends on factors such as the area at issue, the extent of the reform required, the time span available, etc. Furthermore, it is clear that the accelerated transposition method of referral is not considered an appropriate method in all Member States, whereas transposition by delegation is more generally accepted.

Next, examining the ways in which the Member States try to deal with and overcome the implementation and interpretation problems they are faced with, the possibilities for *ex ante* examination of European legislation have been considered, as well as the use of interpretation aids, recourse to different language versions, reliance on consistent interpretation and direct effect, the use of the preliminary procedure and cooperation between courts or consultation taking place otherwise. As regards *ex ante* examination of European legislation, the national reports show that in some states there are highly developed structures for doing so, whereas in others these are far more restricted or at least less used. In most Member States, *travaux préparatoires* are considered useful tools to solve serious interpretation problems. Generally speaking, the preamble plays the most important role in this regard, but Commission documents may sometimes be used for interpretation purposes. Statements in the Council minutes play a negligible role. Other language versions are also used with a view to solving serious interpretation problems, though not to other ends.

Consistent interpretation has come to the fore as the – extremely important – tool for the national court to solve interpretation problems; reliance on direct effect has appeared less prominent in this regard. As to the use that is made of the preliminary rulings procedure to solve interpretation problems, some Member States can be said to cling more to strict application of the legal criteria imposed by Article 234 EC and the *CILFIT* judgment, while others allow more room for policy considerations in the assessment to refer questions or not, such as delay of proceedings. As a means of solving interpretation problems and of avoiding the referral of preliminary questions – formal or informal – cooperation between courts or the consultation of courts or other persons or bodies does not seem to have developed as yet in the Member States.

No matter how many and how sophisticated tools there are or would be in a legal system to prevent or solve interpretation problems, erroneous implementation and interpretation of the law can never be totally excluded. The logical question that then arises is what consequences should be attached to interpretation errors and what repair mechanisms or remedies should be provided for. *Ex post* evaluation of legislation may be one way to trace and repair such shortcomings. In this regard, some Member States appear to have more developed structures for gaining information on and giving follow-up to national judgments identifying shortcomings in the transposition legislation. Furthermore, some national legislatures may be more inclined than others to attach consequences to national court findings of shortcomings in implementation.

The possibility of obtaining compensation for erroneous interpretation of European law by national courts and legislatures is either provided for by national law and/or recognised on the basis of the *Francovich* and *Köbler* judgments by the ECJ. Yet, concrete cases are still quite rare. Furthermore, the national conditions under which compensation can be claimed may differ. At the European level, the possibility for the Commission of starting an infringement procedure for erroneous interpretation of European law by national courts has been considered as well. This issue still seemed still fairly hypothetical at the time the questionnaire was drawn up; current events demonstrate its reality.[200] The national rapporteurs more or less accepted the fact that the Commission may start an Article 226 EC procedure in such a case, but they are also of the opinion that the Commission should only do so in very serious cases and that such a procedure will be of limited, even symbolic importance only. Some rapporteurs advise against this use.

---

[200] See Chapter 2, section 3.4 and the action the Commission took in respect of the Dutch Supreme Court's interpretation of Regulation 1408/71.

This stock-taking of the most important interpretation problems occurring in the Member States and their causes, of the ways in which national authorities deal with them and of the consequences that may be attached to erroneous implementation and interpretation of European law by national authorities, has brought us to identifying as the biggest challenge ahead: how to achieve a better articulation and tie-up of the European and national legal systems in the European legislative process. The contributions made by the national rapporteurs in this regard have led us to the conclusion that an improved involvement of national authorities in the European legislative process is called for. Against this background, we have presented in Part I the cycle of interconnected European and national law-making, based on the idea of co-actorship. In short, national authorities have to assume greater responsibility and play a more proactive role in the European legislative process and should not consider themselves merely as 'consumers' of the outcome or product of that process. This can make an important contribution to the quality of European legislation.

The solutions and suggestions considered by the national rapporteurs can be brought under three different headings. To begin with, how can the transparency of the European legal process and the quality of European legislation itself be improved; what are the possibilities for advising on European legislation with a view to achieving this (section 2.). Next, when it comes to implementing this legislation, what can be done to reduce the implementation and interpretation problems of European legislation to a minimum; can we develop a system of exchanging best practices between the Member States or formulate starting points for the implementation of European legislation (section 3.). Finally, what changes and improvements can be realised as regards the interpretation and application of European legislation by the national courts, in particular as regards the use of the Article 234 EC procedure? Different proposals with a view to this were contained already in the questionnaire and the reactions to these will be considered, as well as other suggestions that have been made in this regard (section 4.).

2.   IMPROVING THE TRANSPARENCY OF AND ADVICE ON EUROPEAN
      LEGISLATION

What ex ante *examination of European legislation could be useful or desirable? What formal or informal advisory procedure could be useful and in what phase of the European legislative process would advice be most appropriate? What role is there for the Association in this regard?* (questions 1.3.1-1.3.4 of the questionnaire)[201]

---

[201] On existing *ex ante* examination, see Chapter 2, section 2.1.

The first two stages or links of the cycle of interconnected European and national law-making that are established in Part I concern the preparation and drafting of European legislation and the European legislative process as such. An early and active involvement and a broad input of national authorities at these stages of the law-making cycle could facilitate the next two stages, i.e., those of the transposition of European legislation into national legislation and of its application by national courts. An improved *ex ante* examination of European (draft) legislation can make an important contribution to this involvement and input.

Different views have been expressed and suggestions made as regards the way in which *ex ante* examination of European legislation may be improved and on how structures for giving advice on European legislation may be developed. Some of these focus on establishing structures at the national level, others more at the European level. Not all rapporteurs see a role for the Association in this regard. More in general, the necessity is underlined of applying very strictly the subsidiarity principle and the fact that national legislative organs share a common interest with the legislative organs of the EU, with a view to maintaining a good balance between national and European legislation (**Germany**) and to ensuring legislative quality (**Finland**).

As regards the European level, the **Finnish** rapporteur is of the opinion that problems should as much as possible be rectified at the source and the emphasis should therefore be put on raising consciousness about the importance of legislative quality in the Commission and Council Secretariat-General and EP services. In the same line of thinking, the **French** rapporteur is of the opinion that the legal service of the Commission could well fulfil a legislation advisory role, considering also that its advices are quasi-binding. The **Spanish** rapporteur also points to the necessity that the legal services of the European institutions (in particular that of the Commission) apply the rules contained in the Interinstitutional Agreement on better law-making, in order to avoid those legislative problems which are not intrinsically linked to the European legal order. Furthermore, national experts consulted by the Commission at the pre-legislative stage should make sure that the terminology in Commission proposals coincides with that of the Member States.

At the national level, the **Greek** rapporteur proposes the setting-up of a central national organ charged with the coordination and checking of European legislation, both at the time of its development and its transposition and application by the national authorities. National and European authorities should consult this organ, drawing its attention to difficulties regarding compatibility and acceptability of the proposed legislation. The **Belgian** rapporteur thinks that it would be advisable to have a mechanism that allows national consultative organs – comparable to the legislative section of the Belgian Council of

State – to obtain information from the European Commission as to how to interpret particular provisions of European law. Such a collaboration would also allow taking into account those language versions which national organs cannot understand. The **Dutch** rapporteur considers that national courts with a legislation consultative function could have a useful input in the legislative process by means of advice to the national government and possibly even directly to the Council of Ministers or the Commission. This could best be developed first at the national level, given that not all Member States have such courts. In their judicial function, courts could collaborate with a view to enabling a joint input in the adoption process of European legislation. Since such advice on draft legislation raises constitutional concerns or at least is not common in some Member States, it seems advisable to experiment with this nationally first. Such a consultation process should at the latest occur at the stage of the decision-making process in which the national governments play a role.

Some rapporteurs are of the opinion that the Association should seize possible opportunities to give advice on Commission proposals, but that thought should be given to the question of how to deal with the workload such an informal advice procedure would bring with it (**Austria**). According to the **Greek** rapporteur, such an intervention would have to occur at an advanced stage of the decision-making process. The **Portuguese** rapporteur considers that optional consultation on questions that the Council would deem necessary could occur in an informal way and at the Commission's request. The **Italian** rapporteur thinks that the Association could play a role not only at the stage of elaboration of European legislation, as an intermediary of the Commission, but also at the transposition stage, with a view to making the transposition of European law in the Member States more homogeneous. As was pointed out also by the Commission representative at the meeting of the Association in Trier in March 2003, the Commission could consult the Association in an informal way, in particular in controversial cases. Advice of the Association could be given either as the outcome of a meeting or of email contacts between all members of the Association or only a number of them, designated to do so pursuant to a division of competences.

Other rapporteurs have been more hesitant about the Association's role in this regard. The **French** rapporteur thus considers it difficult to conceive that the Association could play a legislation advisory function, given that a number of its members do not have such a function even in respect of national legislation. The **Finnish** rapporteur finds it unlikely that any external advisory body could challenge the political imperative to reach decisions and compromises at the crucial stages of the decision-making process (conciliation between the EP and the Council and the final stages preceding common positions and decisions of the Council). The **Spanish** rapporteur does not deem the creation of a European Council of State viable. Moreover, this would add to the complexity and duration of the decision-making process and would arouse suspicion on the part of the Member States and institutions involved in that process. For the same reasons, it is considered difficult to see what role the Association could play in this regard, which does not prevent national Councils of State giving advice on Commission proposals to their own governments. The **German** rapporteur is of the same opinion, considering that such an advice of the Association presupposes understanding among its members, which in their turn would have to contact their national organisations involved in the decision-making process. The fact that the existing procedures are already too short is deemed to put an end to every initiative of a concerted approach of the members. Furthermore, the Association is not and must not be an advanced council of the Union.

Yet, both the **German** and the **Austrian** rapporteurs put forward the idea of having a group of highly qualified legal specialists or a multinational body of experts (possibly including judges) which is involved in very demanding legislative projects and which could identify those points of a Commission proposal that are of general interest for most national authorities and courts. They could then try to find a European solution incorporating as much as possible the structural elements that the legal orders of the Member States have in common. Advice on fundamental questions could be given already before the Commission issues a legislative proposal and more detailed advice could be given when the Commission has to present an amended proposal or after its first reading in the EP.

The **Portuguese** rapporteur is also of the opinion that the quality of European texts could benefit from prior advice of a consultative organ, but the efficacy thereof is deemed to depend on the creation of this organ in the Treaty and on the determination of the cases in which consultation would be compulsory. Requests for advice should emanate from the Council, on the basis of a proposal in an advanced preparatory stage, close to its final version. Giving advice would be most suitable after studies have been made, the legislative proposal has been drafted and at the time of negotiating the approval among the various governments. The informal consultation would have to coincide with other time limits so as not to prolong the decision-making procedure. Furthermore, it is deemed that the articulation of European law could be improved by studying the difficulties that can be expected to arise in its application in the Member States.

Only the **Italian** rapporteur goes a step further and expresses to be in favour of setting up a European Council of State, representing all legal traditions of the Member States, functioning independently and having consultative competence regarding the quality of European legislation. This could be a meeting place for exchanging experiences and also have an added and symbolic value for the

European legal order as a whole. This institution would have to maintain dialogues with the Commission and give its advice at an advanced stage in the legislative process. The **Swedish** rapporteur points to the fact that the issue of a European Council of State has lately been touched upon by a member of the Supreme Administrative Court.[202] Apart from that, he considers it difficult to see what role the Supreme Administrative Court or the Swedish Law Council could play in the preparation of European legislation.

> *What suggestions have been made with a view to increasing the transparency of European law and the use of* travaux *préparatoires?* (cf., questions 2.1.3-2.1.7 of the questionnaire)

In Chapter 2, section 2.2 it has become clear that transparency and *travaux préparatoires* are deemed of great relevance with a view to improving the interpretation and implementation of European legislation. The national reports also show broad agreement on the necessity of more transparency of the European decision-making process and of greater availability of and better access to *travaux préparatoires*. The following concrete suggestions have been made.

The **Greek** rapporteur thinks it useful to have a database, providing electronic access to the following information:

- the text of the European legislation in force, as well as its history (if the text has been amended, also the text of the old provisions; if amendments are under way, the proposed new text);

- the preamble (of the legislation in force, the old text and the proposed text);

- available *travaux préparatoires* (of the legislation in force, the old text and the proposed text);

- opinions of organs such as the Economic and Social Committee and the Committee of the Regions;

- case law of the ECJ/CFI on the legislation at issue;

- preliminary questions or pending cases on the legislation at issue;

- other European texts/legislation adopted on the same legal basis;

- other European texts on the subject matter at issue;

- in the case of directives, the national transposition legislation;

---

[202] Sandström, *Knocking EU Law into Shape*, CMLRev. 2003, Vol. 40, No. 6, pp. 1307-1314.

- case law of national courts/judicial instances on the issue;

- bibliographic references, in particular case notes.

In addition to this, the **Austrian** rapporteur puts forward the idea of drawing up a guide – possibly by the Association in cooperation with the Commission – containing information for the courts on how to search for and get access to documents such as those connected to a Commission proposal.

According to the **Portuguese** rapporteur, transparency of the legislative process can be increased if an explanatory memorandum accompanies all legislative projects, especially when the Council makes amendments. Furthermore, with each project an impact evaluation assessment should be held, providing a synthesis of the outcome of studies and reports which have been drawn up and shedding light on the resources employed or affected and the results foreseen. The uniform application of European law could also be improved by creating a mechanism that facilitates early information on the *travaux préparatoires* of new legislative acts the Commission is proposing to the national governments and parliaments. In the same line of thinking, the **Danish** rapporteur considers that the availability of *travaux préparatoires* could prevent problems of interpretation if they go beyond a mere presentation of the proposed act and face problems possibly arising out of the text proposed. The **Belgian** rapporteur thinks that the adoption of a final explanatory document, expressing and explaining the differences between the text submitted to the Council and the one that is finally adopted, could improve the comprehensibility of Council deliberations. The **French** rapporteur suggests that the Commission publish in the *Official Journal* an overview of the different points of view it has received in respect of a legislative proposal. Apart from that, the **Portuguese** rapporteur also considers it useful to have a brief summary of the – stage of – infringement proceedings published monthly, on fixed dates, in the *OJ*, even if they did not lead to the start of official proceedings.

3.   ESTABLISHING BEST PRACTICES AND COOPERATION ON
       IMPLEMENTATION

How could cooperation on implementation between the Member States get shape, for instance with a view to establishing best practices and/or developing starting points for the implementation of European legislation? What role is there for the Association in this regard? What availability of national implementation data of other Member States through CELEX or otherwise should be provided for? (question 1.2.8 of the questionnaire)

We have identified the implementation or transposition stage as the third connecting link in the cycle of European and national law-making. What may Member States learn from each other's experiences in this regard and, in particular, how can this be put to the benefit of a better implementation of European legislation in the national legal orders?

The national reports make it clear that there are different views on how to deal with the duty to transpose European legislation and with the lack of clarity in that legislation (in particular directives). They also show that implementation techniques may vary to quite some extent. This can partly be explained by the differences between the national legal systems and, as a result, an adequate synthesis of European rules and already existing national rules may require different solutions in the various Member States. Nonetheless, the question arises whether it would be possible to formulate more general starting points or to establish best practices for the transposition of directives, with a view to improving transposition. Furthermore, a more harmonised approach to transposition may also be beneficial to a more uniform application of European legislation. The formulation of such starting points could also be useful for the acceding countries and possibly give guidance on how to prevent implementation problems such as those encountered by Finland in the area of environmental law (see Chapter 2, section 1).

These best practices could concern in particular the issue of whether in implementation the system and terminology of the directive should be respected as much as possible or whether it would be preferable to maintain the national system and terminology of which the transposition legislation will form part. One could also try to identify the do's and don'ts in implementation, for instance regarding the use of accelerated transposition methods such as transposition by referral or try to set the conditions for such use. Apart from that, best practices could be established on how to deal with state-specific factors that may obstruct or complicate proper transposition (such as the existence of a federal structure), on the use and usefulness of *travaux préparatoires* for transposition and on the exchange of information on transposition.

The latter triggers the question of what exchange of national information could be useful. In general, having more developed electronic databases and easier access to information on the transposition of European legislation in other Member States is welcomed. The **Belgian** rapporteur thus states that having access to a database with both specific and general information on how particular directives have been transposed in the Member States would certainly be useful. Yet, quite some rapporteurs have put the direct usefulness of this information into perspective by pointing in particular to the limitation that all Member States will be in the process of drawing up transposition legislation around the same time. Only by the time the deadline for transposition approaches, the database will be filled with information, which will for most Member States be too late to seek inspiration and will only benefit those who are in delay (**Germany**, **Sweden**, **the Netherlands**, **Spain**). The **Finnish** and **Spanish** rapporteurs also observe that in practice, the draftsmen responsible for transposition may gain a more direct and prompt access to similar information through their direct and informal contacts with their colleagues in the administration of other Member States.

At the same time, however, a number of advantages are mentioned. The **German** rapporteur considers that a timely exchange of proposals for legislation could be useful notably as regards similar problems occurring in different Member States. The **French** rapporteur also thinks that transposition will benefit from easier access to this kind of information, given that French *travaux préparatoires* of transposition acts often already refer to the experiences of other Member States. The **Portuguese** rapporteur considers that in the case other Member States run ahead in transposition, it is very useful to be able to study the solutions they found. The **Dutch** rapporteur is of the opinion that making this data available can be useful as regards those aspects of transposition that Member States have in common, i.e., as to how other Member States have dealt with uncertainties or questions regarding the directive itself. Information on the way in which a directive has been implemented may be less useful.[203] The **Austrian** rapporteur stated that the availability of such data could indeed give clues as to how to understand European law, but that there will be many cases in which even such knowledge would not really solve the issue of whether a specific national provision is in conformity with European law. Moreover, it would also require deep insight into the other legal system to understand whether a particular concept has the same meaning as in the state's legal language. Yet, in many cases the Austrian Administrative Court considers German legislation to examine whether a specific solution might be in line with at least the legislation of one other Member State. Enlarging the scope of such an investigation is considered helpful. The **Italian** rapporteur deems that having access to information on the way of transposition in other Member States could at least attenuate, for instance, the transposition problems occurring in respect of the Sixth VAT Directive. It is also considered that harmonisation and uniform interpretation of European law require permanent comparison and exchange of ideas and information between the Member States. Every mechanism or organ facilitating this is deemed useful.

The **British** rapporteur observes that English courts sometimes express interest in seeing how a given provision has been implemented in other Member

---

[203] But an exception in this regard is the implementation of the public procurement directives.

States. The existence of divergent interpretations in national implementing legislation can be relevant, e.g., to the issue of whether a particular interpretation is arguable, or whether a question should be referred to the ECJ for a preliminary ruling. According to the rapporteur, it is difficult to see, however, how the implementing measures of other Member States could assist in interpreting the underlying provision of Community law. He is also not aware of the extent (if any) to which government departments have regard to the practice of other Member States in determining how to implement a Community act.

4.   EFFECTIVE COOPERATION IN THE PRELIMINARY RULINGS PROCEDURE

4.1   General observations

Next, we come to the fourth connecting link we have established in the cycle of European and national law-making, that is, the stage of the application of European legislation by national courts. National courts have to consider themselves increasingly as courts of European law, and with a view to realising this, the cooperation and symbiosis between the ECJ and the national courts needs to be facilitated. Obviously, the preliminary rulings procedure of Article 234 EC is of crucial importance in this respect. The different possibilities to improve the functioning of this procedure will be dealt with in this section.

The preliminary rulings procedure is based on a concept of cooperation which presupposes a separation of functions between the national courts and the Community courts. The national courts have to decide on the facts of a case; the ECJ does not have the jurisdiction to rule on the facts. The ECJ has the final responsibility when it comes to the interpretation of Community law; national courts have a more limited role in this respect. The preliminary procedure thus forms the hub of the system for the correct and uniform application of European law in the national legal orders.

The combination of the need for uniform application of European law and the exclusive power of the ECJ to rule on the interpretation and validity of EC legislation poses the problem for national courts how to know when to refer preliminary questions. This was discussed during the colloquium in Helsinki in 2002. Two other developments were also identified at that colloquium, which are responsible for a continuous flow of references for preliminary rulings and are thus putting pressure on the preliminary procedure. First, there has been an enormous increase in the scope of EC/EU law, both in terms of the fields influenced by this law and in terms of the intensity of this influence (and hence also of the complexity of the law). Second, the enlargement of the European Union will result in even more cases being referred to the ECJ. The findings of the

previous colloquium of the Association thus show that Austria has referred almost 200 cases since it joined the EU in 1995,[204] and Judges Puissochet and
Timmermans of the ECJ state, in their report for this colloquium, that it is not
inconceivable that some courts of the new Member States will follow the example set by the Austrian courts. Judge Meij of the CFI adds to this, in his
report for the present colloquium,[205] that the new areas of law that have now
come within Community competence, such as penal, civil, and migration law,
often contain elements that are at the heart of the national legal traditions,
which makes it even more urgent to find effective mechanisms to deal with the
different national approaches in order to overcome inevitable interpretation
problems.

Concern about the functioning of the preliminary procedure in a Union of 25
Member States provides a new reason to reconsider the present system, given
that throughput time of the procedure now already is sometimes too long.[206]
Furthermore, as Judge Meij observes, there are also inherent limitations to a
jurisdictional decision-making process in which 25 legal traditions are represented and which meet in 20 different languages and it is thus impossible for
the Community courts to realise an output that would be comparable to that of a
national jurisdiction. The expectation seems justified that unchanged use of the
preliminary procedure will lead to unacceptable delays. So, in order to prevent
that the preliminary procedure becomes a victim of its own success,[207] it is
necessary to look at the possibilities for change or adaptation of its present use.

Pursuant to the Nice Treaty, some modifications have already been provided,
such as the possibility to declare the Court of First Instance competent to hear
and determine questions referred for a preliminary ruling in respect of matters
provided for in the Statute of the Court of Justice (Art. 225(3) EC). The possibility of review by the Court of Justice is left open in order to guarantee uniform application of Community law. Such an internal division of tasks could be

---

[204] See the contribution of the Court of Justice to the Helsinki 2002 Colloquium of the Association, 'Le renvoi préjudiciel à la Cour de justice des Communautés européennes', p. 3, available at <www.raadvst-consetat.be>.

[205] This report was written and distributed under the responsibility of its author and all the
views expressed in it are personal views. Cf., also his contribution to the symposium on 'The
Uncertain Future of the Preliminary Rulings Procedure', organised by the Dutch Council of State
in The Hague on 30 January 2004, entitled 'Effective preliminary cooperation: some eclectic
notes'.

[206] According to the report submitted by Judge Meij, in 2003 this was on average 25 months,
the shortest treatment being completed within 3 months and the longest only after 44 months.

[207] This concern was already expressed during the colloquium in Helsinki and is also shared
by Judge Meij in his report to this colloquium. It should also be noted that, since the mid-1990s,
there have been 220 to 250 references each year, which amounts to half of the total number of
proceedings brought annually before the Court of Justice.

a useful filter in the sense that the Court of Justice need only consider the more fundamental issues of Community law. According to Judge Meij, the reflection on the possibility provided by Article 225(3) has not yet sufficiently matured to develop concrete proposals at this moment. Still, he thinks that it seems only logical to confer a preliminary competence on the CFI, at least in those areas in which it rules in principle in last instance, the direct appeals being conferred on a specialised tribunal as envisaged, for instance, in the area of industrial property. Such a conferral of preliminary competence upon the CFI would be justified more by considerations of useful structure than by considerations of decreasing the workload of the ECJ. Judges Puissochet and Timmermans observe that, for the moment, the ECJ has decided not to propose the conferral of part of the preliminary competence to the CFI, given that the new architecture of the Community jurisdiction does not leave sufficient room to the CFI to take on this task on top of the direct appeals and the appeals against the decisions of the 'judicial panels' (or 'specialised courts') it will have to deal with. Still, they consider that, whenever such a conferral becomes possible, it could relieve the ECJ considerably.

Judge Meij also points to another modification introduced by the Nice Treaty, i.e., Article 225A EC which provides the possibility to create 'judicial panels', in Article I-29 of the Constitutional Treaty referred to as 'specialised courts'. In his view, it would seem logical to use this provision for the creation of specialised, first instance courts in the area of competition law and the Community trademark. If this were to be realised with some urgency in the near future and if this were to be coupled with the conferral of preliminary competence on the CFI in the same areas, he thinks that this could release the necessary capacity for an adjustment of the preliminary procedure along the lines set out below in the next subsection.

From the discussion in the next subsections, it will also become clear that Judges Puissochet and Timmermans are not in favour of radical amendments to the present structure of the preliminary procedure, but rather of developing further the reforms of certain provisions of the Rules of Procedure with a view to improving the rapidity and effectiveness of handling cases. These reforms have already produced excellent results.[208] It seems also a shared conviction today that it is by modest but repeated and progressive modifications, based on experience, that productivity can be increased considerably. Judges Puissochet and Timmermans also stress that the Court itself stimulates the use of the preliminary procedure, as a result of its very restrictive interpretation of the notion of 'purely internal situation' and by accepting to interpret internal law provi-

---

[208] See the modified version of the Court's Rules of Procedure, OJ 2001, C 34/1.

sions that refer to Community law provisions. In doing so, the Court has clearly indicated that it wishes to amplify the effects of the preliminary reference and to guarantee a full scope of Community law.

Yet, other options have to be explored as well. In this respect, it has become increasingly clear that structural changes as a result of the 2004 IGC are not to be expected, as the Constitutional Treaty does not propose any modifications to the preliminary procedure.[209] Fundamental changes to the preliminary procedure system that require a Treaty amendment thus seem to be excluded in the short term. A more realistic approach would therefore be to focus on those options that the national courts and the Community courts can put into practice themselves and which contribute to smooth cooperation between them and to an optimal use of the preliminary procedure, thereby reducing the workload of the ECJ.

In the questionnaire, a number of such possibilities regarding the use of Article 234 EC were put forward; they will be discussed in greater detail below. It is important to point out here that the responses of the national rapporteurs show that there are quite some differences of opinion as to the direction or form adaptation of the existing practice should take. Except for the proposal made in question 2.2.6 – viz., that the national court only refers questions if arriving at a decision so requires – there appears to be little agreement in the national reports on the other possibilities mentioned, such as more flexibility of the *CILFIT* criteria or introducing a kind of system of leave to appeal. There is a more solid basis of support for exploring how the *dialogue des juges* can be improved in order to ensure that the national courts apply Community law as effectively and flexibly as possible, without having to have immediate recourse to the preliminary procedure.[210]

At a more fundamental level, the different views that the national rapporteurs have expressed raise the question of how much uniformity in the transposition and application of European law is actually needed. Put differently, when is unity of the law in the EU endangered and what European law issues need interpretation by the ECJ?[211] Not only this question needs to be addressed before considering or reconsidering the various options at the colloquium, but particular attention should also be given to the question whether the same ap-

---

[209] See its Article III-369, which merely adds to the present wording of Article 234 EC that if a preliminary question is raised in a case with regard to a person in custody, the Court of Justice is to act with the minimum of delay.

[210] The development of the Jurifast documentation system, operational since February 2004, can also be seen in this context. See further section 4.8.

[211] Cf., in this sense also Prechal, '*The Preliminary procedure: a role for legal scholarship?*' contribution to the symposium organised by the Dutch Council of State on '*The Uncertain Future of the Preliminary Rulings Procedure*', The Hague, 30 January 2004.

proach should be adopted for both the present and the new Member States. The countries that recently acceded to the EU have witnessed major political, social, economic and legal transformation processes in a very short period of time, hence it is unrealistic (and it would be unfair) to think that they would have to adopt a reluctant approach to the use of the preliminary procedure. Yet, the courts in the 'old' Member States can be expected to rely more on *acte clair* and *acte éclairé*.

Judge Meij observes in this regard that a reassessment of the role and the responsibility of the national jurisdictions in the cooperation process may be inevitable with a view to safeguarding the effective functioning of the preliminary procedure. He also regrets that the European Convention has not seized the opportunity to insert, in Article III-274 of the proposed Constitutional Treaty,[212] a provision confirming the competence of the national courts to apply EU law in the exercise of their competences according to national law. The obligation Article I-28 imposes on the Member States to create rights of appeal which ensure effective judicial protection in the area of EU law is of a different nature. In Meij's view, the creation of such a European legal basis for the role of national jurisdictions would go far beyond being of a merely symbolic value. Seeing its role confirmed in the Constitutional Treaty, the national jurisdiction would be endowed with a proper responsibility and, in a way, mobilised for the effective application of European law. Such a confirmation is considered the more important, given the weakened form in which the obligation of Community loyalty imposed by Article 10 EC reappears in Article I-5(2) of the Constitutional Treaty. According to the Court's case law, the Community role of the national courts is based on this obligation.

4.2   Flexibilising the *CILFIT* criteria

> *With regard to the* CILFIT *judgment, some flexibility could be appropriate, for example, through the introduction of a kind of* de minimis *rule. Perhaps this is risky in connection with the fundamental nature of the preliminary procedure, both for the effect and effectiveness of Community law and for the legal protection of private individuals.* (question 2.2.5)

It can first be reflected upon whether the *CILFIT* criteria on the duty to refer preliminary questions to the ECJ could be liberalised in some way, which would entail that national courts assume a more important role in the application and

---

[212] In the latest version of the Constitutional Treaty (CIG 87/04), Art. III-369.

interpretation of Community law.[213] Advocate-General Jacobs suggested in this respect that the ECJ exercise restraint in dealing with details and that the national courts exercise greater restraint in referring questions for preliminary rulings.[214] From various sides, the proposition has also been put forward that a legal basis should be created in the EC or the Constitutional Treaty confirming the competence of national courts to act as *juge communautaire*.[215]

The **Austrian** rapporteur first wondered what is to be understood by a *de minimis* rule. He considers that it should not matter whether the case itself is of high importance or not, and that a *de minimis* rule would only make sense if it is to be applied with respect to the importance of the question of Community law; what should be decisive is the importance of the question for the implementation of Community law. The question should be of a general nature and touching upon the effectiveness of Community law. In fact, thus he also raises the question of how much uniformity is required.

Some rapporteurs rejected this idea, for different reasons. The **Greek** rapporteur thinks it a premature step at the moment. The **Dutch** rapporteur is of the opinion that there are already methods in practice that can be said to make the introduction of such a *de minimis* rule superfluous (see Chapter 2, section 2.5.1). The **Portuguese** rapporteur is of the opinion that introducing this possibility would affect the legal protection of the rights of individuals. Moreover, it is pointed to the fact that quite some important judgments touching upon fundamental European law aspects have been rendered in cases in which the question in the concrete case could be considered of rather minor importance (in the same sense the **Belgian** rapporteur). The **Swedish** rapporteur observes that the *CILFIT* judgment makes it necessary for the national courts to handle the preliminary procedure with a fair amount of common sense. In the interest of not overloading the system, courts must abstain from asking questions that are not necessary for the adjudication of pending cases. The **Spanish** rapporteur deems it not necessary to loosen the *CILFIT* criteria as this has already occurred in practice; national courts do not always observe the limits of the *acte clair* theory and abstain from asking preliminary questions even if other judges of the same Member State uphold a different interpretation of a particular European

---

[213] See also section 7.2 of the discussion paper, op. cit., n. 3.

[214] F.G. Jacobs, 'The Quality of Community Legislation – What Is to Be Done?', in: Kellermann et al., *Improving the Quality of Legislation in Europe*, Kluwer, 1998, pp. 13-17. See also Court of Justice of the European Communities, information note on references by national courts for preliminary rulings, at <http://www.curia.eu.int/en/txts/others/txt8.pdf>. In point 7 of this note, national courts are asked not to refer until the national proceedings has reached the stage at which the factual and legal context of the question can be determined and both parties have been heard.

[215] See in this sense, e.g., Judge Meij in his report for this colloquium.

law provision. Given the practice of administrative judges in France, the **French** rapporteur does not see any scope for reducing the number of preliminary questions. The practice of referring to case law of the ECJ is considered a factor that already contributes to the reduction thereof, but only to the extent that the national judge is convinced that the ECJ would not come to a different conclusion if asked again. The **Belgian** rapporteur thinks that it is not opportune to introduce a new exception to the *CILFIT* obligation, arguing that it would be difficult to establish what must or could be qualified as a question of little importance. He further considers that if such a rule were to be established, the ECJ should check the use national jurisdictions make of it, if only to avoid that the Commission starts infringement proceedings because of wrongful interpretation of Community law.

Others have been more receptive to this possibility. The **Danish** rapporteur considers that some flexibility would be appropriate since preliminary references may cause substantial delays. In deciding whether or not to refer, the national court should consider the importance of uniform application of European law and of the legal protection of private individuals as well as the opinion of the parties who may want to avoid substantial delays. The **German** rapporteur does not think that loosening the *CILFIT* criteria would decrease the cooperation of national courts with the ECJ as the increasing 'interwovenness' of the economies of the Member States entails that a question arising in one Member State today will present itself in another tomorrow. So, a looser preliminary procedure would not undermine its foundations.

The **British** rapporteur observes that the *CILFIT* rule purports to relax the Article 234(3) obligation on courts from whose decisions there is no judicial remedy to refer questions of Community law to the ECJ. In reality, however, it is considered to relax that obligation hardly at all. Article 234(3) courts are told that they may decide for themselves questions which are *acte clair*, but this will be so only if the national court 'is convinced that the answer is equally obvious to the courts of the other Member States'. The rapporteur thinks there is force in the argument (floated in 2000 by the pre-Nice Reflection Group) that the *CILFIT* criteria are too strict, though he appreciates that, on one view at least, their relaxation would require the repeal or amendment of Article 234(3). The obligation on Article 234(3) courts to refer all interesting or difficult questions of Community law may be considered objectionable for two reasons. Firstly, it prevents those courts from adjudicating in a timely manner in the full range of cases affected by Community law. If they had a discretion to refer, they could legitimately take into account such factors as the limited general importance of an issue, and the likely impact of a delay upon the parties. The latter factor will become particularly acute as Community law extends its reach further into the field of justice (including criminal justice) and home affairs. Secondly, it prevents those courts from realising their considerable potential to contribute to the development of EC law. More subtly, by removing from supreme courts the task of adjudicating difficult issues of Community law, it diminishes the perceived importance of such expertise at lower levels of national judiciaries. The relaxation of the Article 234(3) obligation is presumably said to be 'risky' because of the danger that, without it, some national supreme courts might decide Community law cases in bad faith, or in defiance of established principle. The rapporteur does not believe, however, that Article 234(3) – which lacks teeth of its own – would be capable of deterring a national supreme court which was set upon such a course. Now that substantively incorrect supreme court decisions can trigger both an action for damages and infringement proceedings against the Member State in question, it is hard to see the necessity for Article 234(3) in its present form.[216]

4.3   Referral only if a decision so requires

The national court only refers questions if arriving at a decision so requires (question 2.2.6)

The national reports show much agreement on the rule that only questions should be referred to the ECJ if arriving at a decision so requires. The **Portuguese** courts and the **Dutch** Council of State already apply this rule in practice,[217] as does the **Belgian** Council of State. The **German** rapporteur considers this rule to be perfectly in line with the German notion of jurisdiction to the service of claimants. The workload of the ECJ also imposes such a practice. The **Luxemburg** and **Spanish** rapporteurs also deem this the right way to proceed. The **Greek** rapporteur considers that if this rule was not followed, in particular by lower judges, the solution would be to train the judges, not to amend the Treaty. In this regard, the Association could actually play a role. If the **Danish** Supreme Court finds that there is no reasonable doubt as to the interpretation of the European law provision at issue, it will refuse a request for reference. To avoid unnecessarily burdening the limited capacity of the ECJ, national courts should in appropriate cases be able to rely on their own interpretations of European law.

The **Swedish** rapporteur holds a somewhat different opinion and does not think that the national court should ask questions only when arriving at a decision so requires. It should also consider whether the answer could be of interest

---

[216] See also the British view presented below in section 4.7 in relation to question 2.2.9 of the questionnaire.

[217] See for examples, section 7.2. of the discussion paper, op. cit., n. 3.

to courts in other Member States. If the question concerns a strictly national problem, there may be no need to have the question answered by the ECJ. The Association could play an important role as an intermediary between national courts in assessing whether their problems are of common interest or not.[218] The **French** rapporteur also considers that this option means that not all contradiction in case law can be avoided, which should be considered to be one function of the preliminary procedure.

The **British** rapporteur observes that the English courts attempt to keep preliminary questions to a minimum, and to restrict them to issues which are necessary to enable them to give judgment. However, a reference will occasionally be made notwithstanding that, if the facts are found in a particular way, the point of law referred will not after all be necessary for the disposal of the case. For example, the *Courage v. Crehan* case was a reference on the short but important legal point of whether a party to an agreement contravening Article 81 (1) can sue the other contracting party for damages.[219] Having received a positive answer, the national court concluded after a lengthy trial that the agreement did not in fact contravene Article 81(1) (a finding which is currently under appeal). Such references are submitted to be justifiable on the basis that, had a negative answer been given by the ECJ, no trial would have been necessary (and perhaps also on the basis that the question referred was of considerable general importance). Furthermore, it can also be counter-productive to restrict the number of questions referred in a given case. Sometimes, questions of Community law which are relevant to the case but did not form part of the original reference for a preliminary ruling turn out to be less obvious than had originally been thought. The undesirable consequence may be a second reference (as in *CILFIT*).

4.4   Introducing a 'filter' mechanism

Introducing a 'filter' mechanism: the highest national courts assessing cases before submission to the ECJ? Would this entail amendment of the Treaty? (question 2.2.7)?

---

[218] This observation also illustrates how the perceived aim of the preliminary procedure affects the evaluation of the proposals for adapting it; the Swedish rapporteur clearly holds the view that the main aim of the preliminary procedure is uniform application, not so much the legal protection of the individual. See also Chapter 2, section 2.5.

[219] Case C-453/99 *Courage Ltd v. Bernard Crehan and Bernard Crehan v. Courage Ltd and Others,* ECR [2001] I-6297.

Judges Puissochet and Timmermans observe that, given the objective of the preliminary procedure to ensure the uniform interpretation of European law, it would seem incompatible with the structure of the preliminary system to prohibit a national jurisdiction to turn to the ECJ when confronted with a true interpretation difficulty of European law. In practice, this would then require the parties to appeal the decision that was taken, in order to bring the matter before a court that is competent to make a preliminary reference. They consider that a filter mechanism would not have this disadvantage, but the ECJ has already argued at an earlier stage that such a mechanism can not be reconciled with the principle of mutual cooperation between the national jurisdictions and the ECJ which characterises the preliminary procedure.[220] Still, Judges Puissochet and Timmermans are of the opinion that conferring the power upon the ECJ to assess the expediency of preliminary questions referred to it presents too many advantages to simply abandon this idea. In certain respects, the question is whether the simplified procedure mechanisms introduced into the Court's Rules of Procedure and which the Court proposes to reinforce were not already inspired by such 'filter' logic.

The **German**, **Portuguese**, **Spanish**, **Belgian** and **Italian** rapporteurs reject the possibility of a 'filter' mechanism, observing that it would increase the workload of the national supreme jurisdictions in return for a very small profit for the ECJ, and might even prolong proceedings (also **France**). The **British** rapporteur also strongly opposes such a suggestion, which would, in his view, be wasteful of time and of the resources of the parties and of the courts. The **Austrian** rapporteur expresses doubts about the feasibility of such a system. The **Portuguese** rapporteur observes that such a system might lead to too much emphasis on the national points of view to appreciate European law questions, and to their making their way into the ECJ discussions. With a view to reducing the number of ECJ judgments, it is deemed preferable that the ECJ itself applies a filter mechanism. According to the **Danish** rapporteur, this option may raise substantial procedural problems, in particular concerning the involvement of the parties in the procedure before the higher court. The **Luxemburg** rapporteur is of the opinion that a reform of this kind would negate the very significance of the preliminary procedure, which is to guarantee uniform interpretation of European law, which can only be achieved by having a single institution for this. The **Spanish** rapporteur considers that it would affect the lower courts' awareness of having to act as *juge communautaire*. Moreover,

---

[220] See its report on the future of the jurisdictional system of the EU, submitted to the Council on 10 May 1999.

the preliminary procedure enables these courts to act with more confidence and authority when they have to propose solutions that are contrary to national law.

The **Greek** rapporteur points to the fact that this solution was already rejected in the reflection document of the ECJ, transmitted to the Council on 10 May 1999, because of the risks it entails for the uniform interpretation and application of European law. The **French** rapporteur is of the opinion that this option is only useful if it is demonstrated that numerous preliminary references made by lower courts are in fact uncalled for. The French government also issued a negative opinion on a limitation of the jurisdictions entitled to refer preliminary questions and to a filter system. Yet, lower jurisdictions can make use of the procedure provided for by Article L.113-1 of the Administrative Code, which allows for a non-binding advice of the Council of State on serious interpretation problems. The Council has three months to consider the issue; meanwhile, proceedings are suspended.[221] The **Belgian** rapporteur is of the opinion that this option is detrimental to the development of a European legal culture within the national jurisdictions, as it would make them less responsible as to their role of being first Community judges, acting under the control of the ECJ. His main argument against this option is that such a centralisation at the level of the Member States would lead to 'renationalising' an important part of the legal control of European law, which would result in numerous divergent interpretations from one Member State to another.

Only a few Member States see advantages of this solution. The **Finnish** rapporteur is of the opinion that the role of the national supreme courts is crucial and increasing in European law matters and that at present they are the only courts that have the power and also the obligation to filter the cases to be sent to the ECJ. Since the highest courts normally have good capabilities of handling European law cases, it is considered advisable to strengthen their role in order to unburden the Court of Justice. Under certain conditions, the **Dutch** rapporteur also considers it an option, in particular in the case that the highest national court would obtain proper responsibility in the interpretation of European law; that is to say, if the highest national court were no longer obliged to refer a preliminary question, only in relation to secondary legislation. It would then become a kind of extension of the ECJ. Only in fundamental cases, preliminary questions would have to be posed, which would obviously lead to a decrease of the workload of the ECJ. It is deemed that the risks which this option involves of a certain 'nationalisation' of European law and hence for maintaining the uniformity of European law could be mitigated if the highest

---

[221] For an example, see EC Section, 26 February 1993, *Caisse régionale de crédit agricole mutuelle de Savoie*, No. 143039, p. 37, and Advice of 4 February 2000, M. Mouflin, p. 29.

national courts and the ECJ were to cooperate in an organ in which the ECJ has the possibility to correct the national courts or to invite them to refer preliminary questions. For inspiration, one could also look to the procedures provided for in Article 225 EC – regarding the relation between the ECJ and the CFI – with a view to ensuring unity and consistency of the law. A combination with the option mentioned under question 2.2.9 of the questionnaire could also be considered (see Section 4.9.).

4.5   The national court providing an answer

Could the referring court be obliged to make an analysis of the case itself and formulate an answer to the preliminary question (question 2.2.8)? Does this require a Treaty amendment?

Judges Puissochet and Timmermans observe that introducing a mechanism that would oblige the national jurisdiction to submit its judgment to the ECJ with a view to verifying whether it has given the right interpretation to European law would be objectionable for the same reasons as the procedure that was already evoked in the Court's report of 1999 but not retained. In proceedings before national courts which are not obliged to refer questions to the ECJ and which may thus render judgment in cases which raise issues of Community law, this procedure created the possibility for the parties to demand the submission of the national court's judgment to the ECJ if its interpretation of Community law was disputed. Introducing such a procedure would transform the cooperation between the national jurisdictions and the ECJ into a hierarchical system in which the Court would not just give a preliminary ruling, but render judgment in a concrete case which falls in principle within the competence of the national jurisdiction.

In the national reports, again, pros and cons have been put forward regarding this option. On the one hand, the **Danish** rapporteur considers it not recommendable that the referring court should be obliged to formulate an answer to the preliminary question it poses. Under an adversarial procedure, the national court cannot give such an answer without having heard the opinion of the parties and under Danish law courts do not give advisory opinions. The **Italian** rapporteur is of the opinion that it would increase the workload of the national supreme jurisdictions in return for a very small profit for the ECJ. It could only be useful if it would not be established as a legal obligation, but rather as forming part of the dialogue that takes place between national courts and the ECJ.

The **Belgian** rapporteur is of the same opinion, stressing that it should not be made a condition to the admissibility of the reference. The national judge may not only be in a situation of true perplexity regarding a problem of interpretation of European law,[222] but preliminary questions may also touch upon the construction of the European legal order and imply political jurisprudential choices that only the ECJ can make. The rapporteur refers in this regard to the *Inter-Environnement Wallonie* case,[223] concerning the duty to take account of a directive between the date of its adoption and the date that Member States must have implemented it.

The **British** rapporteur also doubts whether the formulation of an answer to the preliminary question to be referred should be made an obligation. Referring courts which wish to express a view on the questions referred already do so.[224] To require all national courts to express such a view is considered to be wasteful of time and resources in a case where the need for a reference is obvious but the answer to the questions referred is not. It would also expose national courts to the risk of criticism if their analysis was not followed by the ECJ, contrary to the principle that the relationship between national courts and the ECJ is cooperative rather than hierarchical, based on the recognition that each court has a different function.

The **Austrian** rapporteur doubts whether such an obligation could speed up proceedings, as it is considered likely that orders for reference will take longer since finding the right question can be considered to be the really tricky thing with European law. It is also pointed to the Advocate-General's task to provide a concise analysis of the case and to formulate an answer. Again referring to the ECJ's document submitted to the Council on 10 March 1999 on the future of the jurisdictional system of the Union, the **Greek** rapporteur rejects this possibility as it jeopardises the uniform interpretation of European law. The **French** government is also against such a reform, whereas the Council of State has not taken position on this as yet.

On the other hand, in some jurisdictions the formulation of the possible answer is already common practice to a certain extent. In **Luxemburg**, questions are thus formulated in a way that they can be answered by 'yes' or 'no', or two or more alternatives are suggested. This way of operating is perceived as satisfactory. In **Germany**, the judgment for reference may contain the appreciation of the referring court, but most of them do not mention or are limited to some remarks on this. If the ECJ were to desire a more profound appreciation, this would be possible without a Treaty amendment. An explanation for the hesitation of courts to express their own point of view is deemed to lie possibly in a

---

[222] See, for instance, C.E. (section d'administration), *Housieaux*, 1 April 2004, No. 130.058.
[223] Case C-129/96 *Inter-Environnement Wallonie ASBL v. Région wallonne*, ECR [1997] I-7411.
[224] See, e.g., Case C-414/99 *Zino Davidoff SA v. A & G Imports Ltd and Levi Strauss & Co. and Others v. Tesco Stores Ltd and Others*, ECR [2001] I-8691.

wrong understanding of the role of the ECJ, which is to be considered as an aid to and partner of national jurisdictions, not as a higher placed court.

The **Spanish** rapporteur also thinks that this option does not require a Treaty amendment. Even if the Supreme Court prefers putting forward different possible solutions without taking position on these, nothing prohibits other national courts from doing so. Yet, it is considered uncertain what benefits this option holds. The **Portuguese** rapporteur considers that this option could be further explored, as it could self-regulate the reference of questions and facilitate the task of the ECJ. **The Netherlands** is in favour of national judges formulating answers to cases as well, but this does not always occur.[225] It may speed up cases, but 'precooking' them may also lead to a focus on certain aspects only and losing those inviting a different approach out of sight. Moreover, if the national court expresses its view on the case, the party that has been ruled against will do anything to take the edge of the national court's viewpoint. The ECJ then runs the risk of becoming a kind of appeal court.

4.6   Introducing a 'green and/or red light' approach

In line with the suggestion discussed in the previous subsection, Judge Meij more specifically proposed the idea of introducing a green light approach, perhaps even a red light approach. More in particular, he is of the opinion that, given the Court's functional orientation towards safeguarding the unity and the coherence of Community law, its task in the framework of the preliminary rulings procedure is not to provide information on the state of Community law necessary for the solution of each individual case in which a question of Community law is raised before the national court. Preliminary references are not declared inadmissible for this reason, but Article 104(3) of the Court's Rules of Procedure enables the Court to adopt a reasoned order following a simplified procedure instead of adopting a judgment following the regular procedure. The simplified procedure can be followed where a question is identical to a question on which the Court has already ruled, where the answer to such a question may be clearly deduced from existing case law, or where the answer to the question admits of no reasonable doubt.[226] The number of cases in which this provision is now applied does not exceed 10 per cent of the total references made. Meij considers that, to the extent to which effective individual legal protection falls to the national jurisdictions, the examinations that need to be made to solve the

---

[225] Cf., Case C-418-419/97 *ARCO*, ECR [2000] I-4475 and Case C-72/95 *Kraaijeveld,* ECR [1996] I-5403.

[226] See also section 4.9 for the view of Judges Puissochet and Timmermans on the use of this procedure.

conflict in these cases which are dealt with by reasoned order fall in reality within the responsibility of the referring jurisdictions. The question then arises how the obligation to refer for the court ruling in last instance fits in with such a functional orientation of the preliminary procedure. In this context, Meij discusses two recent and more or less complementary approaches.

The first one was proposed by Günther Hirsch, a former member of the ECJ and now president of the German *Bundesgerichtshof*. He argues first of all that the division of functions between the Court and the national jurisdictions, expressed by the dichotomy interpretation/application, is not adequate for determining the conditions under which a preliminary reference is necessary.[227] He considers it more useful to focus on the objectives of the preliminary rulings mechanism. In this perspective, a preliminary reference is only required when: 1) divergent interpretations of Community law exist or may exist in the Member States and may lead to factual situations being treated in a different way; 2) the national jurisdiction encounters difficulties in the interpretation of a Community law provision that is pertinent to the solution of the conflict; 3) the state of Community law requires a jurisprudential development or; 4) a lacuna in the legal protection of individuals has to be filled. Hirsch is of the opinion that not the text, nor the structure or finality of Article 234(3) EC are opposed to limiting the obligation to refer to those situations, thus exceeding the criteria resulting from the *CILFIT* case law. Meij considers this approach to be close to the functional orientation he suggests, to the extent that the second and fourth categories mentioned above are not of an autonomous nature in relation to the first and third categories, which refer to the notions of unity and coherence of Community law. More in particular, he argues that the specific interpretation problems of Community law envisaged in the second category arise either from the lack of familiarisation with Community law (which has to be overcome by other means than having recourse to the preliminary procedure), or from the interpretation of Community law in the framework of the first and third categories.

The second – restrictive – approach was advocated by Advocate-General Francis Jacobs, and proposes to limit the Court's answers to preliminary questions to expressing general orientations which permit the referring jurisdictions to appreciate the facts of the case in view of the applicable Community provision.[228] An interpretation going beyond the analysis of the general criteria for

---

[227] G. Hirsch, 'Das Vorabentscheidungsverfahren: Mehr Freiraum und mehr Verantwortung für die nationalen Gerichte'. In: Colneric et al., *Une communauté de droit, Festschrift für Gil Carlos Rodriguez Iglesías*, Berlin 2003, p. 601.

[228] F.G. Jacobs, 'References to the Court of Justice – the way forward?' In: Colneric et al., *Une communauté de droit, Festschrift für Gil Carlos Rodriguez Iglesías*, Berlin 2003, p. 639.

application of a Community provision, directed in particular to the facts of the case at issue, may leave doubts as to whether this interpretation can be generalised and may thus provoke new detailed questions. The development of jurisprudential frameworks for the appreciation of individual cases by national jurisdictions, however, may leave more scope for dealing with preliminary questions on the basis of the simplified procedure and by adopting reasoned orders. Up to now, it seems that the case law does not yet express a very consistent approach in this regard.[229]

The two discussed approaches do not go so far as to refuse preliminary references that do not fall within the orientations they set out. As such, they cannot be said to ensure a substantial reduction of the average duration of preliminary references. Under these conditions, Meij thinks that the question imposes itself as to whether and to what extent a reassessment of the role of national jurisdictions in the organisation of the preliminary cooperation mechanism may contribute to an increased effectiveness of the system. He argues in particular that the classical conception of the division of competences within the framework of the preliminary procedure is at the origin of the quasi-structural inconveniences of this procedure as it has been conceived up to now. This conception is that the interpretation of Community law falls within the competence of the Court, whereas the establishment of the facts and the application of the Court's interpretation to the case at issue fall within the competence of the national jurisdiction.

According to Meij, the distinction between the interpretation and the application of the law seems to be an obstacle to the effective functioning of the procedure in at least three respects. First of all, the preliminary reference is in fact a somewhat artificial intervention in the decision-making process of the national courts. This process, which encompasses two closely linked aspects, i.e., the coherent search for the pertinent facts and the appropriate interpretation of the applicable legal rules, is cut into two parts which fall within the competence of two distinct jurisdictions. Besides the risks of incomprehension and mutual misunderstanding this entails, pertinent interpretation questions do not necessarily present themselves halfway the reflexion. Secondly, the distinction between interpretation and application is not suitable for making a precise

---

[229] In this regard, Judge Meij points to the contrast between, on the one hand, the judgment in Case C-206/01 *Arsenal v. Reed*, ECR [2002] I-10273, proposing a concrete non-sollicited application of the interpretation developed in this case and, on the other, to the judgment in Case C-40/01 *Ansul v. Ajax*, ECR [2003] I-2439, leaving the sollicited concrete application to the referring jurisdiction. The jurisprudential framework developed in the latter case could subsequently be used in the order of 27 January 2004 in Case C-259/02 *La Mer Technology Inc. v. Laboratoires Goemar SA*, not yet reported.

delimitation of the respective competences of the two jurisdictions. Thirdly, this conception may raise the false impression that the responsibility for the coherent development of Community law lies exclusively with the ECJ. Therefore, with a view to the effective functioning of the preliminary procedure, Meij considers it preferable that the national jurisdiction completes the decision-making process in the case to be referred, by submitting to the Court a full appreciation of the case which includes the interpretation of the applicable Community law. By taking the analysis to the end, almost in the form of a judgment deciding the case, the referring jurisdiction is in the best position to identify the relevant interpretation questions. He further thinks that the risk of the national jurisdiction giving a wrong interpretation of Community law is not of major importance, when compared to the risk of receiving an incomplete answer to a question which, after all, does not appear to be pertinent to the solution of the case. Abandoning the classical distinction would enable national courts to fully assume their responsibility to apply Community law, while recognising the Court's interpretation authority.

Making preliminary references to the ECJ in the sense described above would open up the possibility for the Court to make a selection of the cases that need full treatment from the perspective of unity and coherence of Community law and of the cases that do not pose such a problem and that therefore can be referred back to the national court, having been given the 'green light'. In this way, national courts would be more involved in the development of Community law and they would enable the Court to find a well-considered balance between, on the one hand, the requirements of the unity and coherence of Community law and, on the other, the available resources and the procedural constraints of the submitted cases. In an initial, rather experimental stage, these 'green light' decisions could take the form of an order on the basis of Article 104(3) of the Court's Rules of Procedure. Such an order could merely state that nothing opposes the proposed solution. Even though such an order would not perhaps constitute an authoritative interpretation, it could be exchanged between the different national jurisdictions.[230]

Meij is of the opinion that this would not require a Treaty amendment and that national courts could orientate themselves towards adopting such an experimental 'green light' approach. Furthermore, this still leaves open the possibility for national courts which do not yet consider themselves sufficiently equipped for adopting this approach – possibly those of the new Member States – to opt for the classical method. It would also enable the ECJ to develop a

---

[230] Judge Meij points to Case C-342/01 *María Paz Merino Gómez v. Continental Industrias del Caucho SA*, judgment of 18 March 2004, not yet reported, as an example of a case that could have been dealt with by a green light decision.

certain experience as regards finding a selection mechanism. Yet, with a view to ensuring the full effectiveness of this green light approach, a modification of Article 104(1) of the Rules of Procedure is called for in the sense of limiting the number of languages into which the reference decision should be translated to one or two. For the medium range, amendments of the Rules of Procedure and perhaps of the Statute would be necessary, in particular with a view to formulating the selection criteria on the basis of the acquired experience and to creating a regulatory foundation for such a system.

In the long run, it could even be envisaged to reverse the system, by fixing a deadline for the selection of cases that need an ordinary and complete treatment. The expiration of this deadline without a 'red light' being given would then mean that the decision submitted by the referring court can be applied. In any event, it is considered that a 'green light' system based on an active participation of the referring courts would enable these to fully assume their co-responsibility for the effective treatment of cases requiring the application of Community law, and this within a reasonable time span. Meij further underlines that the approach he advocates requires an adequate equipment of the national jurisdictions (see also section 4.8).

4.7   Introducing a kind of system of leave to appeal

A system in which decisions of the national court are taken and, subsequently, the ECJ has the opportunity during a certain period of time to take a decision on the judgment. A system of leave to appeal could also be considered. (question 2.2.9)

The green and/or red light approach advocated by Meij also bears much resemblance to the following possibility presented in the questionnaire, namely, to introduce a kind of system of leave to appeal or a system whereby the national court decides and the ECJ may react within a certain period of time. This is considered an option only in the **Portuguese** and **Dutch** reports (as regards the latter, see the discussion of the option in relation to question 2.2.7 in section 4.4) and to some extent in the **Belgian** one. The **Portuguese** rapporteur deems this yet a better option than the one explored above, as it would not emphasise any dependence on or functional link between the national jurisdictions and the ECJ. The **Belgian** rapporteur thinks that this option might remedy a wrongful interpretation of Community law, but that it should not replace the preliminary rulings system. He also argues that it may lead to having yet more judicial layers, as there must be an authority considering the necessity of obtaining a Court ruling.

The **Luxemburg** rapporteur considers that the second proposal of a system of leave to appeal is not different from the present system, in which the European jurisdiction is consulted prior to the national court that has to take a decision in conformity with EU law. The **British** rapporteur sees some limited merit in this suggestion, though only after national appeal rights have been exhausted without a reference, and only as a *quid pro quo* for the repeal of Article 234(3). Lord Slynn has suggested that the Commission could have a power to refer aberrant decisions, if sufficiently important, directly to the ECJ. Alternatively, the ECJ itself could have the power within a short time scale to call in a case (in the same way that it will be able to undertake an 'exceptional review' of preliminary rulings by the CFI under Article 225A EC), such a power to be exercisable on its own motion or on petition by the Commission, a Member State, and/or a disappointed litigant. Petition by a disappointed litigant would equate a 'leave to appeal' system. Still, in view of the other remedies discussed in section 4.3 in relation to question 2.2.5 of the questionnaire on flexibility of the *CILFIT* criteria, the rapporteur is not convinced that the advantages of such a system would outweigh the drawbacks.

Opposite views are based on the idea that introducing such possibilities would create legal uncertainty (**France, the UK**) and constitutional problems (**Denmark**). The **Greek** rapporteur here also points to the risks for uniform interpretation of European law. The **Austrian, German, British** and **Spanish** rapporteurs are of the opinion that these options would even increase the workload of the ECJ and that they could harm the dialogue between the national courts and the ECJ. The **Spanish** and **Swedish** rapporteurs take the view that any system in which the ECJ would give its ruling after the national court has expressed its view on the issue in question would change the relationship between the national courts and the ECJ. The latter would turn into a superior court within a hierarchy of courts comprising both national and European courts, whereas at present there is collaboration and division of labour, though not a hierarchical relationship. This should or could not be changed. As to the first option mentioned in question 2.2.9, the **Luxemburg** rapporteur sees only disadvantages, *inter alia*, longer delays and the insolvable problem of detecting the cases that require *a posteriori* intervention. The **Italian** rapporteur states that one must first wait and see whether the *Köbler* judgment will lead to increased use of the preliminary procedure. If that is the case, then it may be useful to consider the idea of having national courts elaborate texts that might decrease the workload of the ECJ. Yet, the idea to leave it to the ECJ to choose the most important cases to deal with seems foreign to most of the European legal systems except for the common law systems. According to the **French** rapporteur, a system of leave seems to contradict the aim of improving the clarity and transparency of European norms. The solution for tackling the delay of proceedings should rather be sought in a structural reform of the Community courts themselves. Procedures could be rationalised, *inter alia*, by having cases of less importance dealt with by only one judge. The **Belgian** rapporteur is of the opinion that, apart from this option, the solution to the present problems has to be sought in particular in procedural adaptations and adaptations of the functioning of the ECJ itself.

4.8 Improving contacts between the highest national courts and the ECJ

How to improve cooperation between national courts and with the ECJ? (question 2.2.10) Should there be an informal or institutionalised network of contacts between the highest national courts and the ECJ? (question 2.2.4) What role would there be for the Association in this regard?

In section 2.6 it was established that, overall, informal or institutionalised forms of cooperation between national courts and between national courts and the Community courts do not appear developed in the Member States. The national reports show a sufficient basis of support for intensifying this cooperation, but the form in which this would have to get shape is a matter for debate. Different views have been expressed on the idea of establishing a network of specialists. The national reports agree on the need for regular meetings of the Association and the need for improving its existing database.

Generally speaking, it seems that there is a preference for some form of informal network over an institutionalised network (**Luxemburg**, **Denmark**, **Portugal**). The **Austrian** rapporteur further is of the opinion that such an informal network could broaden the legal evaluation of a problem and as such facilitate the determination whether or not to refer it to the ECJ. The **Portuguese** rapporteur thinks that the establishment of an informal network of contacts could be very useful and could take the shape of personal consultation. The **Greek** rapporteur expresses a preference for an institutionalised network including the national supreme jurisdictions and the ECJ/CFI, which could enhance the dialogue between judges and facilitate not only the work of the national courts but also that of the European institutions. According to the **Luxemburg** rapporteur, an institutionalised network would require a Treaty amendment. He also states that there are reasons of principle that argue against institutionalising such a cooperation, as the judge has to rely foremost on his own knowledge and experience of the law and on the elements that have been submitted by the parties. Informal consultation of those who are close to European legal practice, including the European institutions, should be possible, however, with a view to facilitating legal examination and to find out about possible precedents in the case law, making a preliminary question superfluous.

The **Danish** rapporteur is of the opinion that a network of specialists may not be particularly necessary at this point in time.

Apart from that, the **German** Federal Administrative Court and the **Greek** rapporteur encourage the establishment of an informal system of information exchange between national courts (both lower and higher) with a view to exchanging information, e.g., on what preliminary questions are envisaged, in order to avoid that another court asks the same questions. The **Swedish** rapporteur deems that a network of contacts between the national courts could be of value, with a view to determining the questions in respect of which there is a common interest. He is more doubtful about whether the national courts should discuss the question with the ECJ.

Regarding the possible role of the Association in this regard, the **Portuguese**, **German**, **Greek** and **Luxemburg** rapporteurs start by underlining the importance of regular meetings of the Association, which may also organise meetings between national courts and European law experts dealing with general and specific European law issues. More specifically, the **French** rapporteur observes that the Association seems willing to give shape to dialogues between judges, by facilitating already existing contacts between all the jurisdictions involved in the application of Community law. Recent case law of the French Council of State shows its willingness to cooperate in such a network.[231] The efforts of the Association concerning publications and databases could be intensified. The **German** and **Austrian** rapporteurs also deem that the Association could serve as a 'clearing point' for all those who desire to get into contact with another court or council of state concerning a specific question. This could be done through regular meetings. The **Portuguese** rapporteur values the idea of having a network of specialised experts, but considers at the same time that this is difficult to realise because of the means that it would involve. Yet, it is suggested that the Association list specialists of different sectors and states, a list which could be contacted through the Internet. Lists could also be drawn up with addresses, etc., of technical assistance services and information and documentation departments of the members of the Association. The **Luxemburg** rapporteur puts forward that a network of specialists could consist of a group of *référendaires* of the national jurisdictions in the area of European law. In this respect, the **German** rapporteur points to the necessity for the new Member States to get acquainted with the mechanism of *dialogue des juges*. The quick and up-to-date dissemination of all European law questions and their interpretation by national courts will entail a decrease in the number of cases in which

---

[231] See the Case *Société Techna S.A. et autres*, Council of State, 29 October 2003, No. 260768.

European law is applied wrongly and will also decrease the need for compensation means for violation of European law by a national jurisdiction.

The **Dutch** rapporteur considers the decentralisation of maintenance of the uniformity of European law necessary with a view to overcoming the workload of the ECJ and to keep the system effective. The options discussed above in relation to questions 2.2.7 and 2.2.9 of the questionnaire are deemed adequate for this. In order to make such a system work smoothly in practice, a network between national courts and the ECJ is deemed useful for the exchange of case law and other developments. The Association could play an instrumental role in this respect, even though it must be observed that not all highest national courts are involved in this. The **Finnish** rapporteur observes that since formal adjustments of the preliminary system are not feasible or desirable at this moment, it should be tried to improve the dialogue by developing the possibility to consult the Court of Justice at the stage in which the national court is considering the necessity to pose a preliminary question. As the preliminary procedure is a dialogue between judges, it should not be characterised by too excessive formalities. The Association could play an important role in this context. The **Italian** rapporteur is no advocate either of formal changes to the system, but points to channels such as the Association. Reducing the workload of the ECJ should preferably be done by reducing the number of preliminary references through the use of paralegal means rather than through formally adjusting the Article 234 procedure – a system which up to now has functioned perfectly –, which would moreover entail major difficulties. Those paralegal means include instruments that permit an improved exchange of information on the transposition and case law of the Member States and create a lively, intensive, continuous debate between lawyers, administrators and legal practitioners of the EU Member States.

Such instruments could naturally include the use of databases. In this respect, the **Luxemburg** Administrative Court and the **Portuguese**, **German** and **Finnish** rapporteurs stress the importance of the database of the Association,[232] and also of improving it by adding new judgments and presenting them in a more complete and uniform way. The latter also observes that the members of the Association could put in more effort to collect and send the relevant decisions of their institution. More information on pending cases and the case law of the ECJ should also be realised. It is in the interest of the national courts and the Court of Justice that national courts have easy access to this information, also with a view to a correct use of the preliminary procedure. The **British** rappor-

---

[232] The website of the Association is hosted by the Belgian Council of State <www.raadvst-consetat.be>.

teur also underlines that a database giving access to full-text judgments on Community law of the higher national courts in all Member States is a most useful tool for judges and practitioners alike. Ideally, there would be at least a summary of each judgment in one or more widely-understood Community languages. This enables national courts not only to compare notes and learn from each other's approaches to a common problem, but also to identify those cases in which divergent interpretations have been given by the courts of different Member States, a factor which may point towards the need to make a reference to the ECJ.

The **Belgian** rapporteur observes that the Belgian Council of State is in favour of setting up an informal or institutionalised network, in which it would like to continue to play an important part. He refers, in this respect, to the Internet site of the European Association of Councils of State and Supreme Administrative Jurisdictions, which already contains the following information: a PDF version of the Information Bulletin of the Association; the proceedings of the Colloquia of the Association; an electronic database now containing some 17.000 references to national decisions touching upon European law, references to notes and comments in legal doctrine; case law of the ECJ; the 'Jurifast' system, containing the references and full text of 'preliminary files' (including the preliminary questions that have been referred, the answer of the ECJ, and the national follow-up decisions) and of other national decisions on the interpretation of Community law in which no questions were referred; and a guide to preliminary proceedings before the ECJ. The cooperation between the ECJ and the national supreme jurisdictions could be developed further by having even more systematised databases containing both European and other relevant case law of the national supreme jurisdictions. Human, financial, and material resources should be made available to this end and, for example, for appointing a correspondent in each jurisdiction, responsible for updating the databases and for exchanging information or responding to requests for information. This should be managed by a secretariat, functioning under the supervision of a scientific committee composed of delegates of the Councils of State and supreme administrative jurisdictions. A legal forum uniting national and European traditions could also be established, maintaining contacts with the legal services of the Community institutions and with the ECJ. It could also be interesting to organise an annual meeting between delegates of each member of the Association concerning a directive that is being prepared, in order to confront the different points of view thereon and the problems posed by the proposal in each of the national legal systems. Such a meeting could also take place after a directive has been adopted.

Judge Meij observes that the existing equipment and infrastructure of the national jurisdictions for submitting a complete analysis and a proposed solution for the Community law problem in the case to be referred varies considerably from one Member State to another and even within Member States. Networks between magistrates are being developed, through associations or periodic conferences. Substantial investments will need to be made in the further development of such networks in order to ensure the management and the exchange of information, possibly in close connection with the documentation and research departments of the Court. In this respect, the possibility to recruit national magistrates as national experts in the service of the Court also deserves attention. The development of networks as well as centres of expertise could lead to a secondary system of coordination, enabling the resolution of many questions that now overburden the primary system of coordination, that is, the preliminary procedure.

4.9 Other possible solutions, in particular reorganisation of the Court's procedures

Other suggestions for possible solutions? (question 2.2.11)

To conclude, the options discussed above are not meant to be exhaustive and other proposals for change can be thought of. At the symposium on 'The Uncertain Future of the Preliminary Procedure', organised by the Dutch Council of State on 30 January 2004, a number of other ideas were discussed, including the following:

- reorganisation of the Community courts and their procedures;

- introduction of specialised courts (see Article III-359 of the Constitutional Treaty);

- submission to the ECJ of questions relating to secondary legislation only;

- replacing the preliminary procedure by direct appeal of the parties to the ECJ in standard procedures;

- regionalisation or decentralisation of the Community courts (having different courts throughout the EU dealing with preliminary questions).

Some of these ideas were touched upon in particular in the report submitted by Judges Puissochet and Timmermans.

Regionalisation

The latter option was also put forward in the Court's report of 1999 on the future of the judicial system in the EU. It was argued in particular that such a system could prevent the blockage of the preliminary procedure as a result of the necessity of translation, by allowing these national courts to use the language of the Member States concerned. As Judges Puissochet and Timmermans hold in their report, the main argument against such regionalisation is the risk of Community law become fragmented, whereas its uniform application constitutes a fundamental basis of the EU.

Reorganisation of the procedures and working methods of the Community courts

Judges Puissochet and Timmermans discuss at quite some length the possibilities to adapt the Court's Rules of Procedure and working methods, with a view to enabling the Court to deal more quickly and in a more effective way with preliminary proceedings.

With respect to the Rules of Procedure, they refer first of all to the simplified procedure provided for by Article 104(3).[233] In application of this Article, the Court has decided that this procedure should be started even before the beginning of the written stage. Once it is clear that a case may be dealt with on the basis of the simplified procedure, the Judge-Rapporteur will propose, after having obtained the opinion of the Advocate-General, to either use this procedure immediately, or to first ask the referring jurisdiction whether it wants to uphold its preliminary question.

In the first option, the case will be presented without delay to the weekly general meeting of the Court, accompanied with a draft order. The registrar will then inform the referring jurisdiction of the Court's intention to follow the simplified procedure, after which the interested parties may give their view on this, generally within one month. The information provided by the registrar encompasses in particular the case law on the basis of which the case can be decided or the reasons because of which the case admits of no reasonable doubt. After the deadline for submission of observations of the interested parties has passed, the case will be referred to a group of judges, including an Advocate-General, with a view to the adoption of the order.

In the second option, which concerns in particular the cases in which questions are referred that are identical to questions on which the Court has already ruled, the Judge-Rapporteur will propose to the president that the registrar asks the referring jurisdiction whether it wants to uphold the preliminary question in view of the case law that is brought to its attention. If the referring jurisdiction

---

[233] See also section 4.6 for the view of Judge Meij on the use of this procedure and the cases in which this procedure may be followed.

does not respond or wants to uphold its question, the process for following the simplified procedure will be set in motion.

Given the progress the simplified procedure has already allowed, the Court has considered whether it is possible to further improve and simplify the 'filter' element which the application of this procedure entails. In this respect, it has already proven useful to retain the informal practice of sending the referring jurisdiction a copy of the judgment in a case in which the Court had to rule on an identical question, accompanied by a letter of the registrar asking whether the referring jurisdiction wants to uphold its question. The national court may in fact want to do so, wishing to see the further development of a certain jurisprudential position. Still, the Court has recently asked the Council to eliminate the necessity to inform the referring jurisdiction and to hear the observations of interested parties, before being able to respond by way of an order. Judges Puissochet and Timmermans argue that this amendment would emphasise the unilateral nature of the choice of the order and that the sole difference with a filter procedure would then lie in the reasoned nature of the order.

Secondly, they mention the possibility for the Court to request clarification from the national court, provided for by Article 104(5) of the Rules of Procedure. The Court may decide upon this during its weekly general meeting and the request may be done with a view to completing or clarifying the factual and legal context of a preliminary reference. On this basis, it can then be concluded whether the reference is admissible. This possibility has to be distinguished from the one provided for by Article 54a, which permits the Judge-Rapporteur and the Advocate-General to request the parties to submit all such information relating to the facts, and all such documents or other particulars, as they may consider relevant. The use of this possibility requires a reinforced cooperation between the Judge-Rapporteur and the Advocate-General with a view to preventing that they pose the same questions or put forward contradictory demands. Furthermore, these requests may not lead the parties to present a legal qualification of the facts, thereby encroaching upon the role of the judge.

Next, Article 104a is mentioned which allows the President to exceptionally decide, on a proposal from the Judge-Rapporteur and after hearing the Advocate-General, to apply an accelerated procedure in matters of exceptional urgency. Given that, up to now, this procedure has been applied in only very few cases,[234] it is considered difficult to draw any lessons from this. It seems only clear that the Court is of the opinion that the Advocate-General has to be heard in an informal way. Overall, it is considered that the Court proceeds rather care-

---

[234] Case C-189/01 *Jippes*, ECR [2001] I-5689 (reference from 27 April 2001, judgment from 12 July 2001) and Case C-27/04 *Commission v. Council*, not yet reported (reference from 27 January 2004, judgment from 13 July 2004).

fully in this respect and it is also observed that an irrational use of this procedure would lead to delaying the handling of other cases. Puissochet and Timmermans also point to Articles 44b and 104(4) which provide for the possibility to skip the oral part of the procedure, if none of the parties has submitted an application setting out the reasons for which it wishes to be heard.

A last measure that may accelerate proceedings is contained in Article 20 of the Statute and enables the Court to render judgment without the Advocate-General having issued an opinion, when the case does not raise a new point of law. Practice shows an increasing use of this possibility.

In an ongoing reflection on its own working methods, the Court has also developed proposals with a view to accelerating and rendering the procedures more effective. The Court has thus proposed to draw up the *rapport d'audience* in a more schematic way, no longer requiring a detailed presentation of the arguments of the parties, thereby limiting the preparatory and translation work. Furthermore, it has proposed to present the viewpoints of the parties only very summarily in the judgment itself, referring instead where necessary to the opinion of the Advocate-General. With a view to alleviating the translation burden, the Court has also proposed to notify the full text of the decision of referral only in the language of the case, with a translation of the questions into the language(s) of the Member State concerned. Still, the translation of the full text in the Court's working language, that is, French, will also remain available. Out of the same concern, the Court has decided to no longer publish the full text of each of its judgments. This does not apply, however, to preliminary judgments, which will continue to be published in all official languages. Finally, the Court deems it useful to point out some relevant elements to the national courts for an effective treatment of their preliminary questions. These include a discussion of the relevant facts and arguments as to why the national court considers the preliminary reference to be indispensable. Furthermore, it is also considered that, in most cases, the national court should be able to present the interpretation that it would have upheld itself if it had not felt the need to refer a preliminary question. This practice is already followed by some national courts.[235]

---

[235] For an example, see Case C-446/02 *Gouralnik*, judgment of 30 April 2004, not yet reported, in which the Court has explicitly referred to the observations presented by the referring German *Bundesfinanzhof*.

5.   SOME FINAL OBSERVATIONS ON THE CYCLE OF EUROPEAN AND
      NATIONAL LAW-MAKING, CONNECTING LINKS AND CO-ACTORSHIP

In conclusion, some important points will be highlighted that came to the fore
during the discussions at the colloquium of the Association in June 2004, focusing in particular on what can be labelled as the consequences of co-actorship
in the European law-making process. The idea of co-actorship as such was
quite generally accepted. At the same time, it also became clear that a number
of efforts and changes need to be made in order to improve the functioning of
this co-actorship at the level of the different connecting links.

Connecting link 1: Preparation and drafting of European legislation

The very first question arising in this regard is whether or not European legislation should be adopted at all. In this respect, it is of eminent importance that the
more limited purpose of EU legislation is kept in mind and that EU legislation
is drafted while bearing in mind the value of variety and diversity. This means
that the necessity of new legislation has to be carefully considered and reasoned
in each given instance and that this necessity is taken into account at the very
beginning of the drafting process, for instance, in the *travaux préparatoires*.
Improvements could be made in this process.

Closely connected to this issue is the *ex ante* examination and impact assessment of proposed EU legislation on the national legal systems in general. In
order to be effective and comprehensive, this should be carried out not only at
the European level but also at the national levels. First of all, the European
Commission, especially its legal service, has an important role to play in this
respect. As regards impact assessments at the national level, national parliaments should not only deal with questions of a more political nature, such as
whether proposals for legislation comply with the subsidiarity principle, but
also ensure the control of how European legislation fits into the national legal
system. In this respect, the role of national legal drafting experts has been
stressed, as well as that of judges, legal experts and interest groups.

Several problems were mentioned with regard to *ex ante* review, in particular
the amount of European legislation. It is considered impossible to give full
attention to all proposals, for instance, by the national parliaments. Furthermore, *ex ante* review does not provide a solution for the last minute amendments that are often made to European legislative proposals. The legal services
of the institutions, in cooperation with linguistic experts, should review these
last minute amendments with great care.

The fact that the subsidiarity principle will be included in the new Constitution for Europe, with a new role to play for the national parliaments under the
Protocol on the role of national parliaments in the European Union, should be

taken as an opportunity to make further arrangements as regards impact assessment and *ex ante* review, for instance, in the Interinstitutional Agreement on guidelines for better law-making. This would elucidate and emphasise the role which the various European and national actors play in the European legislative process and contribute to establishing a true sense of co-actorship.

Connecting link 2: The European legislative process

In line with the above observations, it is also clear that the focus in the decision-making process should be on the question of whether core issues have been dealt with, on whether the above-mentioned balanced evaluation as to whether European legislation is necessary at all has been carried out, whether the objective of the proposed legislation is formulated as clearly and as simple as possible and whether it does not regulate more than is necessary. As to this last aspect, it has to be kept in mind that uniformity is often not needed and not even aimed for and that the directive and the regulation are different instruments. Even if the legal basis leaves no choice in the instrument to be proposed, it should at least be ensured that the nature and the contents of the instrument at issue is in conformity with the characteristics assigned to it in Article 249 EC.

Another aspect deserving attention in this regard is the adoption of *travaux préparatoires* in the European decision-making process. The discussions on this have made it clear that they are considered useful, in particular, when implementing European legislation. However, questions about their usefulness have been raised with regard to their interpretative value before the courts. This seems to slightly contradict the observation made in the report submitted by Judges Puissochet and Timmermans, that the ECJ has recently resorted more often to the use of *travaux préparatoires* in its judgments.

Connecting link 3: The implementation of European legislation in national legislation

The above-mentioned stages of the cycle of European and national law-making and the ways in which these are given shape clearly also have an impact on the following implementing stage. For instance, it has been observed that where directives have in fact the nature of a regulation, this may leave the Member States no other choice than a quite literal transposition and interpretation. Even though literal implementation may be considered satisfactory from the point of view of the European obligation to implement European rules within a certain time limit, this may be problematic from the point of view of the consistency of the national legal system and the practical application of these rules in the Member States. Also from this perspective then, the right choice of the legal instrument should be kept in mind in the preparation, drafting and decision-making stages. Furthermore, it has appeared that the use of the same terminology is no guarantee for having the same effect in the different legal systems of the Member States. The use of European terminology and the terminology to be adopted on the national transposition level is further complicated by the fact that European legislation hardly ever falls on national virgin grounds.

Apart from that, it is clear that the quantity of European legislation that has to be implemented in the national legal orders puts the national implementing mechanisms under pressure. This should also be kept in mind when assessing the necessity and carrying out the impact assessment of proposed European legislation. In this respect, it is also noteworthy that implementation problems contribute to an increased workload of the ECJ (25 to 30 per cent of the infringement procedures).

The above also raises another issue, namely, that Europeanisation of a certain field of law is often a gradual process. Initially, it may be logical to stick to the existing national system and terminology. But the question then arises where the turning point lies: when will it be necessary to adapt the national legal system and terminology to the European system and terminology that have gradually emerged and as a result of which the national and the European systems have also gradually floated away from each other? An example of this is provided by the implementation of the VAT Directives in a number of Member States.

One other question that has emerged and that needs further examination is how the way of transposition or the chosen implementation technique actually relates to interpretation problems that later occur at the judicial level. Can it be said that one technique is to be preferred over others from this perspective?

Connecting link 4: Application of European legislation by national courts, in interaction with the ECJ

The national courts play an important role in the application of European legislation in the national legal system and as such they are also part of the European judiciary. They should also consider themselves a kind of decentralised European courts, which underlines their role as co-actors in the European lawmaking process. The preliminary procedure forms the connecting link between the national courts and the European Court of Justice and the way in which this procedure functions is of crucial importance for the national courts with a view to properly fulfilling their role as European courts and thus as co-actors. This procedure is to function as effectively as possible in order to ensure the best possible interplay between the ECJ and the national courts.

Apart from conceivable institutional changes to the system of the preliminary rulings procedure, it is useful to investigate further the methods that the judicial bodies themselves can adopt to allow the procedure to work as effectively as possible. In this respect, it must be remembered that the preliminary procedure is designed in particular to guarantee the uniform application of European law and hence the necessary unity of law in Europe. This also calls for a balanced use of the preliminary procedure in the light of this aim, which should not be hampered by drawing too far-reaching consequences from the Court's judgment in the *Köbler* case that non-referral by national courts may lead to liability of the Member States. With a view to ensuring this, the reasons behind preliminary references should be investigated further. A particular important question is: Where lies the problem, in European legislation, national implementation, national administration, or elsewhere? Furthermore, JURIFAST could develop into a very helpful tool to reduce the workload of the ECJ in preliminary proceedings, by keeping the national courts better informed on national practices in other Member States when dealing with European law. The art of making references and the application of judgments could also be further developed. Another important factor for the future functioning of the preliminary procedure is also how policy on European legislation develops in the coming period, which brings us to the last connecting link.

Connecting link 5: Feedback; Ex post *evaluation of European legislation*

Notwithstanding the initiatives that are already taken at the European level, in particular by the Commission, with a view to improving and limiting European legislation, it would seem that the time has come to put yet more emphasis on codification, restatement and – where possible – simplification of the vast body of existing European legislation than on the enactment of entirely new legislation. The adoption of new legislation requires balancing the need for unification, harmonisation or cooperation, on the one hand, and the interest of maintaining diversity where possible, on the other. Insights derived from the case law of the national courts and from the transposition problems encountered by the national legislatures can provide the required information as to how to strike this balance and to establish where legislative initiatives are actually desirable.

ANNEXES

Annex 1
QUESTIONNAIRE

Questionnaire for the 2004 Colloquium of the Association of the Councils of State and Supreme Administrative Jurisdictions of the European Union: 'The quality of European legislation and its implementation and application in the national legal order'

Preamble

The theme for the 2004 Colloquium was discussed on the basis of the discussion paper that had been distributed earlier at the meeting of rapporteurs in Trier on 24 and 25 March 2003. Following on from that meeting the discussion is currently focusing on a number of specific aspects. One particular point to emerge is that the quality problems arising with European legislation within national legal systems seems frequently to be a matter of interpretation.

These problems are certainly not caused exclusively because the quality of the legislation as such is so much worse than that of national legislation. Rather it is a consequence of the individual character of Community law. The nature and function of European law after all is different to that of national legislation. The European and national legislative and regulatory process is still mismatched. Problems which arise therefore are mainly problems of interpretation when drafting national implementation legislation and when applying or examining for compatibility by the national court. An understanding of the individual character of Community law in comparison to national law is essential to bring national and European law cultures together.

To be able to tackle the problems that European legislation poses for national legislation and courts, national and European legal cultures will have to be brought closer together. This actually involves three successive stages:

- How can interpretation problems be prevented as such?

- How are interpretation problems handled and solved when they nevertheless occur?

- What are the consequences of errors of interpretation that have been made?

The questionnaire is taking these three items as the point of departure. They will also constitute the basis for the General Report that will be drafted once the responses of the national rapporteurs have been received. The main aim of this is to contribute to an improved method of working with the national judicial bodies and an improved interaction of the national judiciaries with the Court of Justice.

This approach entails that some of the questions in the questionnaire which was discussed in Trier in March 2003 have no longer been included. Other questions are being posed again here with a view to ensuring that the final report is complete. Comments that have already been made will be incorporated in the General Report. In addition a number of the questions build on the findings of the Association's colloquium in Helsinki in 2002.

The questionnaire will be sent to members of the Association and to the Court of Justice of the European Community including the Court of First Instance and to the European Commission. A number of questions specifically relate to the legislative process. Possibly the members of the Association who have an exclusively judicial task may want to leave these questions unanswered.

1. Preventing interpretation problems

1.1 *The set of community instruments: hierarchy, simplification, travaux préparatoires and transparency*

The simplification of the system of Community legislation and regulations has been discussed in the context of the European Convention. It is proposed that a limited number of instruments be used and that a hierarchical distinction be made between legislative, delegated and implementing instruments (see also point 3.1.4 of the discussion paper). In addition it is being proposed that the debate in the Council on legislation in future should take place in public. At the moment the drafting of European legislation is not entirely public so that interpretation of that legislation is made more difficult. The following questions are designed to investigate whether the proposed changes can simplify the implementation and application of European legislation in national legal systems.

1.1.1 Does the present lack of clarity on the hierarchy of European legal norms pose specific problems for the national legislature and courts? If so, which?

1.1.2 To what extent can the proposals in the Convention or any other form of simplification and hierarchical classification of the legal instruments of the European Union help to improve implementation and application of these instruments in the national legal order?

1.1.3   To what extent would the differentiation of the legal instruments of the European Union which has also been proposed (open coordination, self-regulation and co-regulation) create new problems for the implementation and application of Community legislation in the national legal order?

1.1.4   Do you expect that transparency of the entire process of drafting of European legislation will improve the implementation, interpretation and application of European legislation?

1.1.5   What contribution would the availability of systematic and complete *travaux préparatoires* make to preventing interpretation problems (see also point 2.1 below)?[1]

1.2   *Implementation techniques; what is the method adopted for transposition?*

The crucial question is how European and national systems of legal norms can be brought into line so that problems of interpretation are fewer. An inevitable fact is that in contrast to national legislation Community legislation frequently does not require uniformity and is designed more to remedy national differences, notably in so far as these constitute an obstacle to the internal market. An important consequence of this – and at the same time a complication – is that national linking mechanisms and systems of implementation will continue to retain their individual character because European legislation allows scope for divergent national approaches to the implementation of European legislation.

Member States can play an important role in preventing problems in the implementation of European legislation. Crucially they must recognise the individual character of Community law and respect it as much as possible. The fact is that many of the problems are rooted not so much in the European legislation itself as the way in which the legislation is dealt with in the national context. The aim of the questions below is to find out the kind of interpretation problems that occur in implementing European legislation in the Member States and the reason for these. In particular we want to know to what extent the problems of interpretation actually arise as a result of a shortfall in the quality of European legislation or are the result of factors in the national domain. Take as an example the fact that in some Member States quite a few problems arise with regard to interpreting the VAT Directives (this emerges for one thing from the

---

[1] Particularly the Commission proposal and the documents and deliberations within the European Parliament and the Council.

number of preliminary questions submitted to the Court of Justice) while none whatsoever occur in other Member States, though in these in turn there are problems with public tendering or environmental law. Certain problems are possibly be attributed to the inferior quality of European legislation which could more readily be blamed on a poor match between the European and national legislative systems and thus on (incorrect or incomplete) implementation legislation.

1.2.1   What do you think about the adoption of the terminology and system of European legislation in implementation? What problems does this give rise to in practice?

1.2.2   Would you prefer to confine implementation to *ad hoc* adaptation with maintenance of the legislative system concerned as long as possible or would you prefer to bring the entire system of national legislation in that field into line with European legislation (see point 5 of the discussion paper where a number of examples relating to environmental protection and VAT are given). Does the one or the other choice in practice result in problems?

1.2.3   Does your Member State use methods for accelerated implementation such as referral and delegation? How often does this occur? What in practice are the pros and cons of the use of such methods?

1.2.4   Could you indicate fields in which specific problems of interpretation have occurred or are occurring in implementation? If so, what kind of problems are these and what is their cause? (see also question 2.1.1).

1.2.5   Could you indicate how the implementation of tax law or environmental law directives has been tackled, in particular Directive 77/388/EEC (Sixth VAT Directive) and the Directive 79/409/EEC and 92/43/EEC (Bird and Habitat Directive).

1.2.6   Did the implementation of these directives encounter obstacles? What do you think were the reasons for this? (see also question 2.1.1 below).

1.2.7   If the problems have been solved how was this done? (see also point 3.1.2 below).

1.2.8   Do you think that national implementation data of other Member States available in CELEX could be used in preparing implementation legislation?

1.3   Ex ante *checking of European legislation*

During the meeting in Trier we looked at a number of ways of incorporating a legal quality test in the European legislative process. One of the ideas discussed which has been put forward earlier was the setting up of a European Council of State or another general advisory body for legislation. However, for this an institutional reform would be necessary which, as a result of the highly divergent national traditions, is not expected in the near future. Other possibilities are the greater involvement of national parliaments and national civil servants in the European legislative process and also of the national Councils of State themselves. This could possibly be done by means of an informal group or by experts *ad hoc*.

1.3.1   What possibilities of *ex ante* examination for compatibility do you think are desirable/useful or necessary? (See for example the Dutch experiment of advice by the Council of State on Commission proposals for legislation discussed in point 4.2 of the discussion paper).

1.3.2   At what phase of the European legislative process would advice be most appropriate?

1.3.3   Do you have any suggestions for the setting up of an informal advisory procedure?

2.   Handling and solving interpretation problems

2.1   *Interpretation methods and aids to interpretation*

The next question that arises is how the national courts should deal with problems of interpretation once these occur in a concrete case. Quite a few differences emerged among the various Member States at the Trier meeting, for example on the point of comparing different language versions of European legislation and the use of the interpretation documents drawn up by the Commission. The questions below relate to the way in which the national courts deal with European legislation or national implementation legislation and notably whether this differs from the method of interpretation or technique that is followed for the interpretation or application of 'purely' national legislation.

2.1.1   Have the problems referred to under 1.2.2 and 1.2.4 occurred in the administration of justice and if so, in what way? How were they solved?

2.1.2   To what extent are interpretations in conformity with directives or Community law used in interpreting national legislation implementing European legislation?

2.1.3   In interpreting European legislation is use made of *travaux préparatoires* (in so far as these are available)?

2.1.4   In interpreting European legislation is use made of documents drawn up by the Commission at a later date?

2.1.5   To what extent is the preamble considered in interpreting European legislation?

2.1.6   In interpreting European legislation is reference made to statements in the minutes of Council of Ministers?

2.1.7   In interpreting national legislation to implement European legislation is reference made to *travaux préparatoires* of that national legislation (explanatory memorandums, etc.)?

2.1.8   Are different language versions used in interpreting legislation? Are the different language versions regarded as a threat for the correct and uniform interpretation of Community law or do they serve to contribute to it?

2.1.9   Are there in your practice other aspects that are important which have not been mentioned above?

2.2   *Cooperation on interpretation*

On the subject of the administration of justice the cooperation of the members of the Association and of national courts with the European Court of Justice was discussed in Trier as was the cooperation between the members themselves and the mutual cooperation between national courts. The conclusion is that the preliminary procedure is under pressure and that that pressure will increase in the future by expansion of the field of work of the European Union, the stepping up of Community law and the expansion of the EU with ten new Member States.

Improved mutual (informal) cooperation can reduce interpretation problems at an early stage. Various suggestions were put forward as well as suggestions for reducing the pressure of the preliminary procedure. We would like to hear your opinion on these suggestions after first of all posing two general questions on the use of the preliminary procedure as such.

2.2.1   Can you indicate to what extent not so much legal as policy consideration affect the use of the preliminary procedure? What we have in mind are factors such as delay (desired or otherwise) of settling the case and the wishes of the parties. Do they have a significant impact on the decision to refer or otherwise? What is the response of the court?

2.2.2   Do you see the point of the preliminary procedure notably in ensuring the general interest of uniform application of Community law or in the – individual – interest of legal protection?

2.2.3   The national court may informally consult contact persons, both at national and Community level before posing preliminary questions to the European Court of Justice. Could you indicate whether and to what extent this is already done in your Member State?

2.2.4   An – informal or institutionalised – network of contacts between (the highest) national courts and the European Court of Justice.

2.2.5   With regard to the CILFIT judgment some flexibility could be appropriate for example by a kind of de minimis rule. Perhaps this is risky in connection with the fundamental nature of the preliminary procedure, both for the effect and effectiveness of Community law and for the legal protection of private individuals.

2.2.6   The national courts can keep down the number of preliminary questions to a minimum by only posing preliminary questions if this is inevitable for the decision in the case (see also point 7.2 of the discussion paper).

2.2.7   The highest national courts could monitor access to the preliminary procedure by assessing cases before they are submitted to the European Court of Justice. They themselves could then handle other cases. Change of the Treaty would be necessary.

2.2.8   The referring national court could be obliged in the preliminary referral to give an analysis of the case itself and to formulate an answer. Change of the Treaty would be necessary.

2.2.9   A system in which decisions of the national court are made and subsequently the European Court of Justice has the opportunity during a certain period of time to take a decision on the verdict. A system of leave to appeal could also be considered.

2.2.10   What role could the Association play in improving mutual cooperation and cooperation with the European Court of Justice such as setting up a databank, setting up networks of specialists, organising meetings, etc.

2.2.11   Do you have any other suggestions?

3.   Attaching consequences to interpretational errors

Despite the efforts to prevent problems of interpretation and to solve them when they do arise, errors of interpretation will always arise. This applies both in the field of legislation and in the field of the administration of justice. For example it may emerge in a case before the national court that, wrongly, no preliminary questions were posed or that an interpretation followed by the national court in the course of implementation is incorrect. The question then is what consequences should be attached to the observation of such errors.

Although there is no question of a hierarchical relationship between the European Court of Justice and the national courts, the priority of Community law above national law must after all be assured.

As to the administration of justice various national and Community mechanisms were examined in Trier which could be used to remedy such errors. We would like to hear your opinion. In addition, in the legislation *ex post* evaluation of European and national implementation of legislation will have to be addressed. The questions below are intended to provide some insight into the importance of evaluation of legislation to combat problems of interpretation.

3.1   *Ex post examination of legislation*

3.1.1   How can we provide for an improved correction of shortcomings in implementation legislation? (See also point 1.2 above). If the Council of State or the national court has noted certain shortcomings in implementation is this picked up by the national legislature and are consequences attached. If so, what consequences?

3.1.2   To what extent and how is note taken in the administration of justice of shortcomings in national implementation legislation, observed by the European Commission or in some other way, for example, incomplete implementation? Do you see any possibility of improving this? Can an authority or agency be designated which periodically reports on this so that shortcomings can be remedied?

3.1.3   In your view what contribution can ex post examination of both European legislation and the national implementation legislation make to an improved implementation and application of European legislation? In the light of this do you think that the present examination, that takes place both at Community and national level is satisfactory?

3.2   *Community and national repair mechanisms*

3.2.1   Ought the European Commission in the case of errors of interpretation by the national courts make use of the possibility of launching an infringement procedure against a Member State for infringement of Community law by virtue of Article 226 EC?

3.2.2   What are the possibilities of obtaining compensation in the case of an erroneous interpretation of Community law, both by the court and by the legislature?[2]

---

[2] See also Case C-224/01 *Köbler*, ECR [2003] I-10239.

3.2.3   Ought there to be a possibility, apart from the existing applicability of
         Article 234 EC, of a specific or higher provision with the European
         Court of Justice to adjudicate on such issues?

Annex 2
ARTICLES I-33 TO I-37 OF THE TREATY ESTABLISHING A CONSTITUTION FOR EUROPE[1]

Article I-33

The legal acts of the Union

1. To exercise the Union's competences the institutions shall use as legal instruments, in accordance with Part III, European laws, European framework laws, European regulations, European decisions, recommendations and opinions.

A European law shall be a legislative act of general application. It shall be binding in its entirety and directly applicable in all Member States.

A European framework law shall be a legislative act binding, as to the result to be achieved, upon each Member State to which it is addressed, but shall leave to the national authorities the choice of form and methods.

A European regulation shall be a non-legislative act of general application for the implementation of legislative acts and of certain provisions of the Constitution. It may either be binding in its entirety and directly applicable in all Member States, or be binding, as to the result to be achieved, upon each Member State to which it is addressed, but shall leave to the national authorities the choice of form and methods.

A European decision shall be a non-legislative act, binding in its entirety. A decision which specifies those to whom it is addressed shall be binding only on them.

Recommendations and opinions shall have no binding force.

---

[1] CIG 87/04, 6 August 2004. In the Draft Constitutional Treaty, drawn up by the European Convention, Arts. I-32 to I-36.

2. When considering draft legislative acts, the European Parliament and the Council shall refrain from adopting acts not provided for by the relevant legislative procedure in the area in question.

Article I-34

Legislative acts

1. European laws and framework laws shall be adopted, on the basis of proposals from the Commission, jointly by the European Parliament and the Council under the ordinary legislative procedure as set out in Article III-396. If the two institutions cannot reach agreement on an act, it shall not be adopted.

2. In the specific cases provided for in the Constitution, European laws and framework laws shall be adopted by the European Parliament with the participation of the Council, or by the latter with the participation of the European Parliament, in accordance with special legislative procedures.

3. In the specific cases provided for in the Constitution, European laws and framework laws may be adopted at the initiative of a group of Member States or of the European Parliament, on a recommendation from the European Central Bank or at the request of the Court of Justice or the European Investment Bank.

Article I-35

Non-legislative acts

1. The European Council shall adopt European decisions in the cases provided for in the Constitution.

2. The Council and the Commission, in particular in the cases referred to in Articles I-36 and I-37, and the European Central Bank in the specific cases provided for in the Constitution, shall adopt European regulations and decisions.

3. The Council shall adopt recommendations. It shall act on a proposal from the Commission in all cases where the Constitution provides that it shall adopt acts on a proposal from the Commission. It shall act unanimously in those areas in which unanimity is required for the adoption of a Union act. The Commission, and the European Central Bank in the specific cases provided for in the Constitution, shall adopt recommendations.

Article I-36

Delegated European regulations

1. European laws and framework laws may delegate to the Commission the power to adopt delegated European regulations to supplement or amend certain non-essential elements of the law or framework law.

The objectives, content, scope and duration of the delegation of power shall be explicitly defined in the European laws and framework laws. The essential elements of an area shall be reserved for the European law or framework law and accordingly shall not be the subject of a delegation of power.

2. European laws and framework laws shall explicitly lay down the conditions to which the delegation is subject; these conditions may be as follows:

(a) the European Parliament or the Council may decide to revoke the delegation;

(b) the delegated European regulation may enter into force only if no objection has been expressed by the European Parliament or the Council within a period set by the European law or framework law.

For the purposes of (a) and (b), the European Parliament shall act by a majority of its component members, and the Council by a qualified majority.

Article I-37

Implementing acts

1. Member States shall adopt all measures of national law necessary to implement legally binding Union acts.

2. Where uniform conditions for implementing legally binding Union acts are needed, those acts shall confer implementing powers on the Commission, or, in duly justified specific cases and in the cases provided for in Article I-40, on the Council.

3. For the purposes of paragraph 2, European laws shall lay down in advance the rules and general principles concerning mechanisms for control by Member States of the Commission's exercise of implementing powers.

4. Union implementing acts shall take the form of European implementing regulations or European implementing decisions.